CW01511827

For my mother Joan Brown, who never doubted me.

after a child dies

parents' grief

JENNI THOMAS OBE
WITH SARAH G. THOMPSON

First published in Great Britain in 2025 by ALMT Publishing, Angus Lawson Memorial Trust, Ravensmere, Cryers Hill Road, High Wycombe, HP15 6LJ www.almt.org

Copyright © Jenni Thomas 2025

Jenni Thomas has asserted her right under the Copyright, Designs and Patents Act, 1988, to be identified as Author of this work.

All rights reserved. No part of this book may be reproduced or transmitted in any form or by any means, electronic or mechanical, including photo-copying, recording, or by any information storage and retrieval system, without permission in writing from the publisher.

Every reasonable effort has been made to trace copyright holders of material reproduced in this book, but if any have been inadvertently overlooked, the publishers would be glad to hear from them.

British Library Cataloguing-in-Publication Data
A catalogue record for this book is available from the British Library

ISBN 978-1-0369-1097-6

Typeset by Fakenham Prepress Solutions, Fakenham, Norfolk NR21 8NL
eBook by Fakenham Prepress Solutions, Fakenham, Norfolk NR21 8NL

Contents

Foreword

Nick Lawson *Founder, The Angus Lawson Memorial Trust*

Our son Angus drowned on 7 September 2006, shortly before his second birthday. Many kind people sent words of sympathy and advice at the time. One of the best analogies for the grief I was feeling came in a letter from a father whose two sons had died. He said: 'It's like walking over jagged rocks with bare feet.' He explained that, initially, the pain is intense and unbearable, but that, although it always remains painful, your feet do harden up and get used to it, and the sharp edges of the rocks get smoother over time.

At the time, I couldn't believe that it would ever feel any less torturous. The visceral, animal pain wasn't the only new challenge I had to face. When your child dies, everything in your life changes, and you have almost no control over any of it; your relationship with your partner, your family, your friends, your work, and every aspect of your day-to-day functioning is stripped down and torn apart. Some days you struggle to understand why you should ever get out of bed. As Claudius says in Shakespeare's *Hamlet*: 'When sorrows come, they come not single spies but in battalions.'

Kara, my wife, and I met Jenni Thomas shortly after Angus died. She was the NHS bereavement counsellor for the Buckinghamshire NHS Trust where we lived, and she supported us unfailingly through the early days and weeks after our son's death. As time passed, we maintained regular grief support sessions with her, both as a couple and individually.

In those early meetings, I would mostly stare out of the window; I didn't want to engage or participate in the dialogue, for fear of breaking down and crying in front of anyone. But Jenni was patient and consistent, and, as time went by, I was able to talk more openly about Angus and the way I felt.

I've learned a lot about this grief from other people whose children have died, and the community of bereaved parents I have come to know since Angus's death has been a source of enormous support and inspiration. Everyone grieves differently, but there are also some common motifs.

Like many of the bereaved fathers I know, I was desperate in my grief to create some sort of order, to make some logical sense of Angus's death. I had a deep conviction that if I could just throw enough positives at this black hole of grief, I would somehow be better able to explain what had happened. It was with this conviction in mind that I founded The Angus Lawson Memorial Trust, a charity with a mission to improve the lives of children and young people around the world. A large part of our work means supporting families with bereaved children or those whose parents are dying. In 2009, Jenni joined the charity to head up our grief support offering and became our bereavement counsellor as well as our dedicated patron. She has been a brilliant cheerleader for the charity ever since.

As I write this, it is hard to believe that almost two decades have passed since Angus died. The promise I was made about walking on those jagged rocks turns out to be true. Nothing can ever make Angus's death any easier to accept, but Kara and I have three more beautiful sons and we have stayed together, stayed in the fight. I think an enormous amount of the longevity we're so proud of and the strength that binds our family is down to the consistent and unflinchingly honest counsel we have all had from Jenni over the years.

I am acutely aware that not every family who suffers the death of a much-loved child is fortunate enough to have access to Jenni or someone like her. And yet I know how desperately important the care you receive when your child dies can be, not only at the time, but also down the years. When Jenni told me she wanted to retire, I asked her if she would write this book, so that some of the experience, wisdom and kindness that helped us so much could be captured for others to benefit from. I hear her voice so clearly in these pages and I am so grateful that she has been able to do this for us, and for herself.

If you are a bereaved parent, I hope her words give some comfort to you and those around you. The journey ahead of you is long and lonely, but I can promise you that you won't always feel so immobilised by your grief. I can also promise you that you will be able to say your child's name one day without crying, and that one day you will be able to share a memory of them and not feel so entirely broken; wistful and sad, yes, but not broken. One day you will realise the jagged rocks of grief have become smooth pebbles, and you will be able to make the same promises of hope to someone else who needs to hear them.

Introduction

'The true way to mourn the dead is to care for the living who belong to them.'

Edmund Burke

The death of a child is cruel. It is the end of life before it has hardly begun; the greatest of gifts given with one hand and taken away with the other. If your baby or child has recently died, or if you know they are going to die soon, and you are reading this, it is likely that you are feeling a sense of overwhelming shock and confusion. Simply taking in these words might seem strange and feel wrong to you at the moment, as though you are not meant to be reading them at all. You might feel that you do not deserve or wish to ever feel better about your child's death than you do now. This is perfectly understandable. There is no need to force yourself to read the pages that follow if you do not feel ready to. They will all still be here when you are. There is no correct procedure or timeline for your grief when your child dies.

Children and babies of all ages die for many reasons: illness and disease, tragic accidents, unexplained deaths, suicide and murder. Sometimes their death is a shock and sometimes you have lived with the knowledge they are going to die for many months. Sometimes parents must make horrifying choices and accept responsibilities about their child's life, and their death – things that they never imagined they would need to do and therefore have no idea how to cope with. This book will not dwell on the events that have led you here. Nor will it tell you how to mourn or promise to cure your sadness. It is here simply to help you carry on in the face of the awful truth you have been left with. The very worst thing has happened to you and, for many parents, it can feel as though it will be impossible to continue with their own lives now that their child is dead. This book is here to help you keep going.

Everything in these pages is informed by many years of learning from and working with bereaved parents, witnessing their experiences and their courage, both at the time of their child's death and throughout the years that follow. Every parent who has loved and grieved for a child finds their own way through this life-changing event. Every family experiences this moment in their way, according to the codes and scripts that have been etched on them by generations before them and according to their own life experiences, circumstances and values.

However, within these pages, you will find suggestions about some of the things you can choose to do now and in the years to come that might be useful. There is often so much regret in the grief for a dead child; a deep sense that if only something had been done differently or someone had behaved in a different way, this awful tragedy might not have happened. And if we are a parent, there also might be a sense of failure – that we have failed in our most important role: that of caregiver. Feelings, too, of ambivalence and even anger might arise, perhaps towards a problematic child or a death that has happened against a background of dispute. These emotions can all feel especially heightened and shameful to us in grief.

No one can prevent these thoughts, feelings and convictions from occupying your mind. Rare is the parent who can ever say with honesty that they do not feel any responsibility, regret or anger for their child's death, even if to an outsider they are clearly not responsible and should not feel any of these things. But approaching these feelings in a way that does not compromise the precious memories you want to cherish can be helpful in the years to come. In my work, I've learned that the way we all talk to and support parents when their child dies can have a profound effect on the way they carry the experience with them through life. I want to share as much as I can here in the hope it will help you on your journey through grief. If nothing else, grief is a process in which we all continue to learn – about ourselves and the world around us – throughout our own lives and the lives of others.

I hope this book will also act as an unfailing friend. Even those of us with the most loving and supportive families and friends can find ourselves feeling oddly unfamiliar, mixed emotions towards those who love us the most at this time. In their efforts to take away our pain, those we consider pillars of our ordinary lives can sometimes become people we want to distance ourselves from in our grief. With emotions running so high, some people feel a strong need to isolate themselves from and reject loved ones who are trying so hard to fix us now that we are so broken. So it is not always the loving grandparents, the doting uncles and aunts, and the best friends, all of them no doubt also devastated by what has happened, who can offer us what we need in this grief. Grandparents, in particular, can invoke hugely complex and conflicting feelings. With the death of a child, the family order outwardly shifts and changes, and yet the child's place in the family remains. The lines between parents and children of all ages in the family script can begin to blur and become difficult to make sense of. This book offers you someone unrelated, without any connections, and a place where you can hear the stories of other parents who have experienced your pain and think and feel all the things you need to without fear of judgement, without a family drama to act out or the burden of someone else's grief to make space for.

It would be wrong of me to promise that you will one day recover from what has happened. However, what the many hundreds of bereaved parents I have worked with over 60 years have taught me is that, over time, you will be able to live in a more peaceful acceptance. And that you will, at some point, want to do this, whether it is for your other children, family members or for yourself. I've also learned from bereaved parents that there is a future in which you will be able to find a way to live with the reality of what has happened and continue to parent and love the child who has died, while also living life without their physical presence, as unacceptable and improbable as that might sound at first.

Despite an enormous amount of progress in the way we approach death and dying, Western culture still does not do it well. Things have improved since I first began working with bereaved parents, but it is fair to say that, culturally, we still feel uncomfortable around the topic. It is as though we believe that if we ignore it for long enough it might go away. Our language around death and the English language around grief reflect this. We talk of people 'passing away' and 'leaving' us, of being 'deceased' and of 'lights going out'. We say anything but 'death' and 'dying' and 'dead'. Facing the reality of what has happened and accepting it is the first and most important part of living any kind of life after your child's death. For this reason, I will try to talk as plainly as I can. You are most likely reading this because your child has died. It is still hard for me to write these words, even after 60 years of working with bereaved families, and I know how extremely hard it is for any parent to read them. And yet it is with the greatest respect for bereaved parents and for the children they love that this honest language is used throughout the book. Honesty, acceptance and natural, genuine communication will carry you through, even though at times they might also leave you feeling more exposed and vulnerable. Using simple, honest language will also permit those around you to talk more freely about your child and everything related to them, now and in the future; I hope this book will also be helpful for people who are supporting parents whose child is dying or has died. It is for everyone who needs it, and when I talk about parents and mothers and fathers, I do, of course, mean parents of all backgrounds and experiences, including step-, adoptive and LGBTQIA+ parents.

I have been lucky to work with some extraordinary people in my career – not only the parents and families whose precious children have died and who have shared their grief, but also the numerous professionals, doctors and nurses, midwives, psychologists, counsellors and other experts who have taught me so much about what families may need in their darkest hour. I have included their stories and voices in these pages as much as possible, to comfort and inspire you.

It is impossible to put children into categories simply by age. Every child is different and means something unique and special to their parents and families. The seams of time and growth in which babies become infants, young children become older children and teenagers become young adults are deep and wide, without clearly defined or officially recognised boundaries. It is no easier to draw these lines in death than it is in life. Therefore, you will find this book addresses three main stages: infancy, childhood and when an older or adult child dies. It is a sad truth that many more babies than children die each year and, as a result, there is a great deal of support and advice available for those parents whose baby has died. It may be that the child you are grieving sits in one section of this book – they may be at the very start of life or on the edge of what we call adulthood. While everyone's experiences are different and no children are the same, I hope that you will find the support and the words that you need to read somewhere among these pages.

Please note: I am enormously grateful to all the parents whose experiences are described in this book; they are a fraction of the many families whose much-loved children and their deaths have informed my work throughout my career. Without them and their willingness to share their stories and feelings, it would not have been possible to write this book. All of the parents and their children I describe are real, although some names and other details have been changed in order to protect their privacy.

About Me

I am often asked how and why I first began working with bereaved families. I think what people really want to know is: what qualifies me to be supporting parents when their child has died? A lot of people make the reasonable assumption that I have experienced the death of my own child. I am thankful to be able to say that I have not been through this tragedy first hand – I have four children and eleven grandchildren; although, very sadly, my granddaughter, baby Annabelle, was born very prematurely and died soon after her birth. However, grief and mourning have been a part of my life since childhood. And, as with everyone, my childhood experiences shaped who I am today, and the work I find myself motivated by.

My family was in mourning throughout my childhood. My father was killed at the end of the Second World War, just after my second birthday. So I grew up in the midst of the grief my mother experienced for him, and for her much-loved 19-year-old brother who died just a few months before my father. I don't remember anyone talking to me, or each other, about feelings of grief as a child, but I will never forget the overwhelming sadness I saw and felt for my mother when I became old enough to understand what had happened. I wanted to make it better for her. I think that's where the nurse and carer in me comes from.

After an early childhood spent in South Africa with my younger sisters Shirley and Lesley, I moved to England just in time for the Queen's coronation. I began my career in the NHS as a nursery nurse in a maternity home, then part of Amersham Hospital, where unmarried women were sent to have their babies, away from public view. It was the 1960s and, sadly, it was still considered shameful for a woman to have a baby outside marriage. Pregnant women, mostly young women from affluent backgrounds, would come to the maternity home to have their babies, who were then adopted. This was an early lesson for me, in the grief felt by any mother who must give up the baby they have carried for nine months.

I also worked as part of the special care baby unit (SCBU) team at Amersham. Like every other healthcare professional in those days, I had no training in how to understand and care for patients whose child had died in hospital. Death tends to happen more frequently in hospitals than most places, and yet none of the medical staff or managers were given any training or support when it came to dealing with bereaved families. Doctors, nurses, staff and managers were simply expected to know how to address such a death and the devastated families it leaves behind. Although we each had our own sense of humanity and caring, staff who showed their emotions were still often considered to be unprofessional. I had a sense even then that the way the NHS approached bereavement, especially the death of a child, was wrong. But it was when psychologist and psychiatrist John Bowlby, the so-called 'father of attachment theory', came to Amersham that I really began to understand what needed to change and why.

One morning, I was told by my ward manager that someone very important was coming to visit us at the hospital for the week and I was to shadow him and help with what he needed. That person was John Bowlby and the week I spent with him was enormously impactful, as I watched him at work and began to understand his theory of attachment. In those days, children in the children's ward were allowed to be visited by their parents for just one hour a day. Bowlby suggested that these poorly and no doubt lonely children would not only benefit from having their parents visit more often, but that they might recover faster with the love and support of their families nearby. This was at odds with the thinking of the ward manager – and of the times in general – who did not want children getting upset and making a fuss when their parents inevitably left. Bowlby suggested that sick children should not be separated from their parents, who could bring in mattresses to sleep on, and argued that a child knowing they were cared for and loved (attachment) was an important part of the human evolutionary will to survive and that denying them of that connection might actually hinder their recovery.

The time I spent with him planted a seed of confidence and certainty in me, that my purpose was to help parents and children, and it wasn't long before I was able to put everything I'd learned with Bowlby into practice. One day at work on the SCBU, a senior midwife asked me if I would help a new mother who didn't want to feed her newborn son. I saw the mother curled up in her bed, barely able to lift her head. When I asked what was troubling her, she explained that she knew she had been pregnant with twins when she came into the hospital. She knew she had carried another baby but she had been given an emergency Caesarean section under a general anaesthetic and, when she woke up after the operation, she only had one baby: a little baby boy. No one had told her what had happened to her other baby; she didn't even know if she'd had a girl or another baby boy.

I knew the medical consultant would not approve of what I did next, but I said to the mum I would go and find out what I could for her. I went down to the hospital mortuary, a temporary mortuary in a Portakabin, and I asked the mortician if a new baby had been brought in that morning. He let me in and showed me a little baby girl, lying in a dish covered with a towel. I went back and told the grieving mum that she had had a little girl. 'She looks very like your little boy. She didn't ever take a breath. No one knows why she died; she was what we call stillborn.'

As was common practice, the dead baby had been taken away without her mother ever seeing her. The pervading belief was that it would be kinder to keep the baby's body out of the mother's view so as not to upset her. But Bowlby had helped me to understand that, whether a baby lives or dies, their mother still feels a deep and lasting attachment to them. In those days, there was never any question that this mother might see or hold her daughter, but I had at least been able to tell her that she had had a daughter. This very sad mum thanked me for giving her this information and, after some time, sat up and allowed me to help her breastfeed her little son.

I continued to work as a nurse in maternity and paediatric units at the Royal Berkshire Hospital in Reading and Wycombe General Hospital on SCBU. Wherever I worked, I noticed that families seemed to be grateful to and comforted by the staff who were able to show their own feelings and say how sorry they were when a baby or child had died. I began to question and challenge bereavement culture within our healthcare system, in particular the separation of medical care and emotional care. I saw very clearly that death and dying needed to be acknowledged as an important part of the care we provide for all families and healthcare professionals. I decided that I would try to change the system from the inside, and my mission to improve bereavement culture in the NHS began.

Initially, I negotiated with senior management, with the help of my then manager Jean Macdonald (a truly brilliant woman and nurse, who went on to receive an MBE), who headed up the SCBU team, to allow me to provide bereavement support for families, giving them time and space in hospitals to share their feelings rather than sending them home in shock shortly after their child had died, as frequently happened. In the 1970s, I devised a training programme that would educate professionals in loss and grief as well as provide emotional support for them while they developed their own self-awareness. A significant and daunting aspect of my work was trying to help healthcare professionals realise that asking for support could be seen as a strength and not a weakness. I also saw first hand how important it was for grieving families to know that the grief they experienced was a normal reaction to an extremely unusual event. Parents told me that what they needed in those moments – that human, caring support – was invaluable.

In 1970, I attended a training conference under the great Swiss-American psychiatrist Dr Elisabeth Kübler-Ross. The residential course was titled 'Living Until You Die', and is an experience that has stayed with me throughout the years, mostly because of the way it was delivered. Dr Kübler-Ross was, at the time, gaining fame for her groundbreaking book, *On Death and Dying*. The 100 participants at the conference were made up of 50 healthcare professionals like me and 50 terminally ill people, and, on the first day, as we all gathered in the lecture hall, none of us knew who was who; who was living and who was dying. I will never forget the sight of Dr Kübler-Ross as she entered the room strumming a ukulele and singing 'Kumbaya My Lord'. As she made her way through the crowd, she encouraged everyone in the room to join her in the song. But as the 'Someone's dying

Lord' verse arrived, half of the audience fell silent. It was, of course, the health professionals who could not bring themselves to sing that line, knowing they were in the company of people who really were dying. Spending that time with and training under Dr Kübler-Ross gave me the confidence I needed to work directly with bereaved parents and families.

During the 1980s, I trained as a counsellor with the Westminster Pastoral Foundation, training which gave me the confidence I needed to offer bereavement support in my role as a nurse. In 1985, I became the first bereavement counsellor working with families in the NHS, working for Buckinghamshire NHS Trust. The success of my work there led to similar posts being created in other health authorities, using protocols and policies I developed. Later on, I gained a diploma from the University of Surrey in humanistic psychology and person-centred art therapy, and continued my work teaching nurses, doctors, hospital chaplains and other medical professionals how to act as advocates for vulnerable, grieving families. The training resources I devised and produced were always based on what I had learned from bereaved families. I continued to develop this work as bereavement facilitator for the Oxford Regional Health Authority.

During this time, Sir Muir Gray, Chief Medical Officer for the Authority, suggested I should establish a charity to take this work forward on a national basis. Working with and supported by my NHS colleagues, I founded The Child Bereavement Trust (now Child Bereavement UK), as an NHS initiative, in September 1994. At the time, the charity was based in my home and my role was fully funded by the NHS. It was launched at the Royal College of Nursing in the presence of Diana, Princess of Wales. In 2000, I was the joint winner of the inaugural Nye Bevan Award for those working in the NHS, an award that will always remain very special to me, because of all the wonderful people I worked with throughout my career in the NHS. I was given the award for pioneering service improvement in the difficult area of neonatal bereavement. In 2001, I was appointed to serve on the Retained Organs Commission (ROC), set up to advise and oversee the return of organs and tissue to bereaved families across the UK. In 2002, I was awarded the OBE for my services to child bereavement, presented by the now King Charles II. And in 2003, I moved from my role as Child Bereavement UK's Chief Executive to founder President, a role I stayed in until I left the charity in the capable hands of Ann Chalmers in 2009. Prince William continues to be the charity's Royal Patron.

During all of this time, I continued my work as a maternity and paediatric bereavement facilitator, funded by the Buckinghamshire NHS Trust until I retired from the NHS in 2008. I am hugely proud to know that the bereavement training model I developed continues to serve as a benchmark for many public services including the police, social services and education. Without the many outstanding professionals I have worked with throughout my career, my work with bereaved families would not have been possible. I also spent time in Singapore, helping the many bereaved expat families whose children and relatives died in the Boxing Day Tsunami in Thailand in 2004. My experience in Singapore taught me that, while there are many cultural differences, the devastating grief parents feel for a child is the same the world over.

In 2006, in my work as a hospital bereavement counsellor, I met and supported Nick and Kara Lawson, parents of two-year-old Angus, after he tragically died. Nick is the founder of The Angus Lawson Memorial Trust (ALMT), the charity behind this book. This was the beginning of a long and meaningful partnership with the ALMT, where, since 2009, I have been working as the charity's grief counsellor, supporting bereaved parents and families. I am also the proud patron of the ALMT and I am hugely grateful to this organisation for funding this book as I retire in my 82nd year.

I also provide support for families when a baby or child dies through Rosie's Rainbow Fund and I am the patron of two other charities: Teddy's Wish and Sudden Unexplained Death in Childhood (SUDC) UK (see the Charities and Organisations section of this book, which starts on page 172, for more information on the work of these and other charities). I'm also an adviser to the Ruth Strauss Foundation, having supported Sir Andrew and his wife in talking to their sons, Sam and Luca, in 2018 about Ruth's then imminent death.

I have written various professional publications, including a chapter on grief and bereavement for the *Mayes' Midwifery* journal, and created a number of training videos including *Death at Birth*, *Grieving After the Death of Your Baby* and *The Danger Age* with producer Brad Williams. In 2022, I created a podcast series, *Jenni Thomas Talks About Child Bereavement*, with Nick Heath, which you can listen to on the ALMT website (see page 171 for the address).

This is my first book specifically for bereaved parents and I am so grateful that you are here reading it. I know it will never change what has happened to you, but I hope in these pages you will find a small amount of the comfort and the courage you need to keep going.

Jenni

There is a list of recommended further reading and organisations that might be useful to you in the coming months and years on pages 172–178.

Chapter 1

Understanding Parents' Grief

'Those who grieve know – they can apprehend the truth of the world because they have been as close to the great mystery as it is possible to be. We understand, in our blood and the blood of our children, that we are defenceless against the vagaries of the world, but that we all have the capacity for extraordinary resilience, especially when it is toughened in the furnace of our rage.'

Nick Cave, *The Red Hand Files*

'The only cure for grief is to grieve.'

Earl Grollman, *Living When a Loved One Has Died*

When we are talking and thinking about a child's death, it can be useful to consider the way grief can be experienced. It may not make it any easier to accept, but it can help us to understand how it affects us in our mind and body. It is always an unfathomable shock when a child dies, however it happens. And, for most of us, it is more powerful and terrifying than any other kind of grief we are ever likely to feel. It can affect us in many ways and on many different levels. Managing such an extreme situation, not knowing if or how you will ever survive it, or why you are feeling and behaving the way you are, can be very frightening. Bereaved parents have taught me that knowing a little more about grief and how others in their situation have felt can, in some small way, be reassuring.

Most of us will experience grief at some point in our lives. As such, it is one of the most common states a human being can find themselves living in, and yet, culturally, it is still so often presented to us as a kind of extended sadness, something to be overcome with flowers and cards and cups of tea. Or else it is treated like an illness, something to be cured with medication and therapy.

Grief can be a great sadness and it can also become something that requires us to seek extra help and support. But it is never only these things, and it is certainly not automatically a psychiatric illness. When a child dies, grief is the natural human reaction to such a distressing event – the profound yearning and longing we feel when we can no longer be with someone precious. For most of us, the most treasured person in our lives is our child or children, so when we can no longer see them or touch them or be near them, their absence is enormously difficult for us to accept, and this can last for years.

In this way, the grief we experience for a child we love is a deep trauma, one that can feel at first like a physical wound, in that it may happen to us suddenly, and be so shocking that it may be too big to believe and take on. In the first hours and days, you may feel and appear to be numb and incapable of expression.

16

This numbness is nature's way of protecting you – a kind of emotional pause button that allows you to become accustomed to the brutal truth of things gradually. In fact, many parents can find the pain of their very early grief becomes increasingly severe as the numbness recedes and the full reality sinks in. It can be some time before the pain of the reality also gradually recedes.

In these early weeks and months, you may also experience some difficulties completing the previously simple tasks of everyday life. You may lose the inclination to interact with people or even to leave the safety of your home. Parents I have worked with have told me that being at home or in another place where you can feel safe, where no one can find you or be around you unless you wish them to be, is very important.

You may lose the need to perform basic self-care such as washing your hair or getting dressed. These things can feel enormously difficult and pointless. You may not feel hungry and, even though you are exhausted, because grief is exhausting, it might be very difficult for you to get to sleep. The overwhelming feeling of grief that hits you as you try to sleep makes you need to get up and do something, to divert yourself. On other days, you might find you need to sleep all day, and getting out of bed seems impossible. Your body and your movements may slow down as you battle the feelings you are trying to manage, or they may speed up as you try to avoid or deny those same feelings. For some, avoiding feelings and forcing themselves to keep busy, to keep going, is important. You may feel unable to do anything or you may not be able to stop doing things. Be reassured that it doesn't matter what you do or how you react, you are simply coping in the best way you can with something you had never expected to have to cope with. There is no right way to grieve; we do as we must.

You might also experience the sense that your child is close by or think you can hear a familiar sound they used to make. You might think you see them out of the corner of your eye or smell something that reminds you of them. These thoughts are common in the early weeks and months; they are not hallucinations so much as your deepest needs surfacing. You need to stay close to your child. Your mind is not yet able to take on the new reality. There is a great deal of searching in grief; searching for someone you love. There is yearning and a kind of unsettled restlessness. This is natural, and can continue for many months and years.

You may find yourself crying instantaneously and for very long periods of time; tears you didn't realise were in you. You may find yourself being triggered to cry by the simplest thing. Seeing other people's children of the same age, even if only on the television or out of the window, can be enormously difficult and provoke extreme distress. When your child has died, it can seem as though the whole world is full of other people's healthy, living children.

Some bereaved parents say they feel like they are going mad. Grief does resemble madness. Some parents have told me they have thought very seriously about digging up their child's body from their grave, even though they know this makes no sense. You forget important things, you can't remember if you did something or not, why you walked into this room or drove home in that direction, why you are holding these clothes, who you last told about your child. People you live with and those closest to you might worry about you and wonder if you are depressed. It's true that in grief there is depression, but it is seldom the kind that needs medical treatment. And if clinical depression is an empty space void of feelings, grief is a room bursting at the walls with them.

Many parents have told me that they feel a new sense of extreme anxiety and doom come over them after the death of their child. Nothing about life and the living feels safe anymore. The world has become a fragile and dangerous place, where something so awful can and does happen. You, too, may feel this unfamiliar sense of vulnerability and fear. Living with this new anxiety is one of the hardest challenges grieving parents face.

> 'No-one ever told me that grief felt so like fear. I am not afraid, but the sensation is like being afraid. The same fluttering in the stomach, the same restlessness, the yawning. I keep on swallowing.
>
> 'At other times it feels like being mildly drunk, or concussed. There is a sort of invisible blanket between the world and me. I find it hard to take in what anyone says. Or perhaps, hard to want to take it in. It is so uninteresting. Yet I want the others to be about me. I dread the moments when the house is empty. If only they would talk to one another and not me.'
>
> **C. S. Lewis,** *A Grief Observed*

It is important to remember that none of this suggests there is anything wrong with you. This is the way grief feels when our most precious person dies. It is awful and no one and nothing can make sense of it. The only thing that is certain about this period of such intensity in the early days, weeks, months and even years is that it doesn't always feel this way. Grief, and the way we feel it, changes over time. But grief can never be rushed. And it may take a great deal longer than you or anyone else might expect to one day notice that it doesn't ache quite so much. It may also feel frightening to imagine not feeling this way; staying with the pain can keep you connected to your child. You might worry that by not feeling things as much or as intensely, you are somehow forgetting them or moving on from something you never wanted to move on from. All of this is normal and understandable. Knowing about and accepting it can help you to take grief's blows as a necessary part of this experience, as painful and wounding as they are.

Attempting to Understand Our Grief

'Bereavement is what happens to you, grief is what you feel, and mourning is what you do.'

Dr Richard Wilson, *An Acquaintance with Death; Memoirs of a Paediatrician*

Many psychologists and experts have studied grief. If you've been to a bookshop or searched online to try to find something to read about what you are going through, you'll know that there are many books containing theories and models around the experience of human grief. Studies and surveys have been analysed and bereaved people observed over time; normal and abnormal behaviours have been defined and redefined. Strategies for working through, dealing with and letting go have been turned into methods and even smartphone apps for so-called recovery. While approaches and definitions vary from expert to expert, and thinking changes over time, the thing they all have in common is a good intention: to place some kind of order around the chaos, to attempt to make sense of life's most senseless event.

In my work supporting grieving parents, they have taught me that grief cannot be described with bullet points, or contained in a neat theory or set of stages. There is no book (not even this one) or theory or app that can offer you a satisfactory explanation or set out a foolproof guide to the grief a parent feels after the death of their child. Even the word 'grief' is not a sufficient way to describe the tidal wave of pain that has hit you and from under which may feel you will never wholly resurface. After all my years working in this field, I still struggle to find the words to describe the sheer enormity of parental grief.

However, I've also seen how many bereaved parents find comfort in the company of other grieving parents, and in the wisdom and insight of those who have attempted to work out why they feel as they do. As a grief counsellor, I've found that the information and insight offered by some books and psychological models, while it cannot ever be prescriptive or definitive, can still provide us with ideas to think about and insight into our state of mind in grief. They cannot take us to shore, but they can offer the tiniest and briefest of life rafts at a time when we find ourselves drowning in an ocean of pain. At the back of this book you will find a list of further recommended reading should you wish to explore the science and psychology behind grief (see page 176).

The dual process model of grief

As we've touched on, many bereaved parents say they feel like they are losing their minds when their child dies. Their entire world has been turned upside down and they can't make sense of anything anymore; they feel unfamiliar with themselves and the way they are behaving. If they have a partner, they can begin to feel very distant from them, especially if the way their partner is behaving and responding seems strange to them. The disconnect between themselves, their partner (or a friend or sibling who is supporting them) and the world outside can leave many bereaved parents feeling like they are out of control and their relationships may never recover. This is especially true in the early stages of grief, but is not limited to this time, and this sense of confusion and unfamiliarity with life and others, as though they are on the outside looking in, can stay with parents for many years, even a lifetime.

Something that I find helpful to share when a bereaved parent is feeling this way is the 'dual process model' of grief, which I learned from the psychologist Professor Margaret Stroebe when she shared it with me after a conference in Hong Kong. I share it here so that you can see if it helps you. You will also notice I refer to the loss and restorative ways of being that Stroebe identified in the dual process throughout this book, as it is integral to the way in which I support bereaved parents.

In 1999, Margaret Stroebe and her partner Henk Schut published 'The dual process model of coping with bereavement'.

In it, they described how people who are bereaved tend to behave in two ways in order to be able to cope: loss-oriented and restoration-oriented behaviours.

Loss-oriented behaviours are mostly rooted in our thoughts and feelings and tend to keep us entirely focused on our emotions in grief. Loss behaviours can include yearning for our child and going through events over and over again, not wanting to move on from grief, being unable to settle or to rest and a sense of being physically overwhelmed and exhausted. Loss tends to be inward-looking and exceptionally tiring. Trying to support someone who appears to be consumed by their loss can also be very worrying for their partner, co-parent, family or close friend. It can seem as though they might never come back to who they once were or be able to return to any kind of normal life.

In contrast, restoration-oriented behaviours are when we attend to life's changes and choose to get on with life. In the early stages, this might be as simple as getting a death certificate and doing the admin around our child's death, telling friends the sad news, sorting out a bedroom, informing authorities of their death or planning a funeral or memorial service. Later on, we might take up a new hobby or throw ourselves into our work. Some people do these things with a vigour that is restorative in its energy. We all need some of this restorative energy, otherwise it is almost impossible to get on with life.

It is helpful to remember that neither loss nor restorative behaviours are better or worse for someone grieving for their child. Loss behaviours are vital; we all need to feel and be sad, angry and devastated when a child has died, and we can encourage people we are supporting to have their loss feelings and do their loss behaviours. Equally, restorative ways of being are important as they can help you attend to life's changes and see a light at the end of the tunnel; the reminder that there is still a life to manage and one day enjoy again. It is only by going to and from the two different ways of being, by moving and oscillating between them, that we are more able to manage grief. They are both equally important in the painful process of grieving.

It may be the case that some men are generally more restorative and women tend to need to stay longer in their feelings of loss, and part of this is about the roles men and women have traditionally played in the family and society. It is not that one is better than the other, but the difference between these ways of behaving can impact both partners, and cause problems and misunderstandings. In my experience supporting couples, it is often those who manage to share and talk together after their child has died, and can not only tolerate but understand each other's ways of behaving, whether loss or restorative, who are more able to be there and support each other in grief. We'll speak more about this in Chapter 6 (page 117) when we look at the parent relationship.

Being aware of the dual process of grief is also very helpful when supporting young people and other children in families, who can appear to be carefree and playful one minute and consumed by sadness about their sibling's death the next. Knowing that this is a typical way to be, and appreciating that both kinds of behaviour are not only normal but necessary in grief, can be very helpful in understanding your own behaviour and that of those around you.

The tasks of mourning

Something else that grief counsellors, including myself, might have in mind when supporting bereaved parents and children are the tasks of grieving. American psychologist William J. Worden first wrote about the four 'tasks' of mourning in his book *Grief Counseling and Grief Therapy*. Worden suggested that by continuing to actively recognise and engage in the grief we are feeling, rather than simply allowing it to happen to us or avoiding it, we can better manage it. Many of the parents I have worked with are comforted by realising that their exhaustion is a result of the huge task that is mourning. The simple notion of their grief being a task can be helpful, because tasks are hard work. There is something about having hard work to do that feels appropriate to their state of mind – a way of doing something at a time when no one really knows where to start. I've shared Worden's four tasks with you below so that you can think about and explore these ideas in the context of your own grief.

Accepting the reality of your loss

Denial of what has happened serves a purpose in that it gives us time to gradually absorb and believe in the truth of what has happened. Parents in denial might want to continue to talk about their child in the present tense or to make plans as if their child was still alive. However, if we continue and get stuck in denial for a long time, it stops us from accepting the truth of what has happened and being more able to move on with life.

Feeling the pain of grief

Death brings up a kaleidoscope of emotions and every person's viewpoint is different. The important part is not what the emotions are, but allowing ourselves to feel them without judgement or shame. Some people turn to coping behaviours such as addictions or avoidance in order to block the pain, but in order to begin to manage life again, our task is to allow ourselves to feel and share our tough and difficult feelings.

Adjusting to a world without your child

There are three main types of adjustments we can very gradually make after the death of a child, says Worden. There are the external adjustments we must make, such as the cancelling of child benefit payments or the swimming lessons or the university application. There are the internal adjustments – these are changes in your identity as a parent to your child. Who are you now that your child is dead? What is your purpose if not to raise your child? And there are spiritual adjustments to consider: what do you believe about life and death now? Is the world still a good place? Are you hoping that one day you will be reunited with your child?

Keeping an enduring connection with your child

Continuing your connection with your child after they have died is a natural way to live life without them. Finding ways to nurture and maintain that connection allows you to feel you have not left them behind while also forming new relationships and moving forward with your life. Many parents continue to do things that are connected to their child and parent their children through kind and helpful gestures, such as setting up a charity. There's more on this in Chapter 8, Continuing to Parent (page 153).

'I still have bad days with the pain of losing Caron, but part of my healing is to help others cope.'

Gloria Hunniford, *The Belfast Telegraph,*
9 October 2014

Grief over time

'It isn't for the moment that you are struck that you need courage, but for the long uphill climb back to sanity and faith and security.'

Anne Morrow Lindbergh, *Gift from the Sea*

Like everything and everyone, grief changes over time. Or, perhaps it is that grief stays the same, and people grow and change around their grief, adding layers of new life that take away the sharpness of the grief that lives inside them. Like a scar, grief will never go away and will always hurt at times, some more than others, but new experiences and moments of happiness and joy will grow around it.

It is not always helpful to make comparisons when it comes to the death of a child, but one I return to when supporting parents is that of the fried egg, a model based on the work of Dr Lois Tonkin. When facing a lifetime of grief for their child and wondering how and if they will ever carry on, many parents find it useful to imagine their grief as a fried egg. Their child's death is the yolk in the centre – it never changes size or shape or colour; it is always there. But the white around it moves, expands and changes shape as the egg cooks. The rest of life is the egg white, changing as you age and growing around the yolk. As hard as it is to imagine in the beginning, nice things do happen again in life. And the pain of what you have been through doesn't dominate your life like it does in the beginning. It never goes away, but you can and do learn to live with it.

Some parents are able and fortunate enough to have another child or children after a child has died and, while they can experience tremendous anxiety and fear around having a new baby, they do go on to love their next child every bit as much as the child they are grieving. (More on siblings in Chapter 7, page 133.) Sadly, not all parents who want to conceive again are able to, and this is an extremely painful experience. If they don't have another child, many parents do still go on to have a fulfilling family life and to manage their grief in ways that feel useful and comforting to them. We will explore the idea that parents can and do continue to parent a child who has died in Chapter 8 (page 153).

Occasionally, something unexpected can force a parent to revisit the pain of their early grief. This might be a sibling having a child who reminds you of your own, for example. Or it might be a friend's child turning 18 when yours might also have turned 18, or the sight of children going back to school in September. It hurts deeply. You might find yourself feeling almost as if the death is happening all over again and experience extreme reactions similar to those you had when it originally happened. This can be distressing because it happens a long time after the event and people around you and medical professionals might suggest you see a therapist or that you have somehow not sufficiently grieved for your child. Although medication can sometimes be helpful, it is very important to find a professional who is comfortable around extreme grief and understands the fragile nature of the events that are unfolding (see page 51 for advice on finding a grief counsellor). With caring and regular support, parents can usually get back on track.

Managing Your Grief for a Child: Some Things You Might Find Useful

The American poet Robert Frost wrote: 'The only way out is through.' While you are going through the very worst time imaginable, go gently with yourself. There are no cures or remedies for the pain of this grief, but there are some common, simple tasks and things to do that many bereaved parents have told me they found helpful on the long road ahead of them.

Take part in the rituals that follow your child's death

Confronting our denial and accepting what has happened is an important task in grief. It might be tempting to hide away and avoid the cultural rituals and necessary arrangements that follow your child's death; the reality of planning a funeral, choosing a coffin or writing a eulogy can feel like too much to bear. But these rituals can also be a way of helping things become real and, in this way, can make your grief more manageable over time. Creating a memorial service or celebration of their child's life is a task no parent ever wants to do, but if you are able to take an active role in them, it will usually be a comfort to know you have done so. Many parents have told me they feel relieved that they managed to arrange a funeral they felt proud of, and even years later they are comforted by the memory of it.

Get out in nature

Being in nature invariably lifts our mood and nearly always helps. You will almost certainly want to close all the doors and windows and pull all the curtains, and that can be a comforting way to be, for a while. But there is also something very soothing and grounding about being in nature, breathing in fresh air, feeling a breeze or raindrops on your face. Even if only for a few minutes, try to get outside if you can – the fresh air and movement will give your body the boost it needs to keep going. The sheer scale of nature can also shift your perspective and help you to feel held by something greater.

Take care around alcohol and other substances

Turning to alcohol or drugs at this time is understandable; it is an easy way of numbing the feelings you don't want to have to feel. But it is only ever a temporary solution and will usually only make you feel worse and can become addictive. It is a one step forward, two steps back solution. If you find yourself relying on alcohol or other substances too much, try to find other ways of managing your feelings if you can. Many bereaved parents turn to exercise as a healthier way of managing; going for a run, doing an online exercise class or even taking a short walk around the block can be a good diversion from the temptation to open a bottle, especially in the evenings when work and other distractions may not be there to catch you.

As in all areas of life, your friends and family will be important in supporting you and a simple phone call when you are feeling lonely can help. Charities such as Frank can give impartial advice on drugs and addiction. Drinkaware.co.uk offers information and support for anyone who is concerned about their drinking or about someone else. More helpful contacts and organisations are listed on page 172.

Practise mindfulness and meditation

Some parents find mindfulness and meditation helpful at times when they feel anxious or overwhelmed. Grounding techniques such as naming your emotions or what you see around you can be very calming when it feels like you are losing control of your thoughts. Breathing exercises and physical practices like yoga or going for a walk in the forest (what the Japanese call Shinrin-yoku or 'forest bathing') are all ways of being present in the moment. Everyone has different needs and things that work for them. Your local leisure or health centre can be a good place to find information on classes and groups that might help.

Something everyone can do at any time to help cope with anxious thoughts and feelings is breathwork. 'Being aware of your breath forces you into the present moment', writes Eckhart Tolle in *A New Earth*. Below is a simple breathing exercise (sometimes called the 'box breathing' technique) you can do right now, or whenever you need, to help alleviate panic and anxiety. Before you begin, try to make yourself as comfortable as possible. Place your arms by your sides or on the arms of a chair and have both feet flat on the ground:

1. Breathe in slowly for a count of four.
2. Hold your breath for a count of four.
3. Breathe out slowly and steadily through your mouth, counting to four.
4. Hold your breath again for a count of four.
5. Repeat three or four times, or until you feel calmer.

Plant something

'In tending a plot and nurturing and caring for plants, we are constantly faced with disappearance and return', writes Sue Stuart-Smith in *The Well Gardened Mind*. 'The natural cycles of growth and decay can help us understand and accept that mourning is part of the cycle of life, and that when we can't mourn it is as if a perpetual winter takes hold of us.'

Planting and growing in memory of someone you loved and watching plants flourish over the years can be very comforting and provide an opportunity to nurture when you are feeling robbed of being able to do so. It doesn't need to be an elaborate garden – it can be herbs on a windowsill or a small pot by the front door. The point is not the scale of your gardening endeavours, but the process of doing it. There is more about gardening for grief in Chapter 8 (page 157).

Find people who understand

Getting involved in something that means something to you or your child often puts you in touch with other parents who understand what you have been through, and means you get to do something that feels positive and restorative when everything else feels pointless. It might be a while before you feel ready to do this, but it can be helpful just to know that you might do it further down the line. Some wonderfully helpful charities and organisations have been set up by grieving parents. We'll explore this further in Chapter 8 (page 162) and there are some charities and organisations you might want to reach out to for support on page 172.

You'll find more suggestions throughout the book about some of the things you can do to help you in your grief.

Other People and the Pressure to Move On From Grief

If your child has died, you may find that those around you, whether family members or friends, find it difficult to know what to say and how to behave towards you.

Death and dying is a subject most people find extremely difficult to approach. When it is the death of a child, you may find that some people simply avoid talking to you or seeing you. This is usually because they are afraid of upsetting you even more with the wrong words or actions. They might also be afraid of what you might tell them. Humans are experts at ignoring things that make them uncomfortable. And the death of a child is one of life's most uncomfortable realities.

Sometimes, when someone does try to comfort you, perhaps with a phone call or a card through the door, you may find that they really do say the wrong words or use the wrong actions. In trying to somehow make things better, not only for you but for themselves, people can say all sorts of things that may feel inappropriate or insensitive to you. If there has been a long illness, people might talk of relief. If there has been a shock death, people might talk of it being quick. If your child was very young, they might try to suggest that they did not ever have to grow up and know the miseries of adulthood, and if they were an adult they might say that they at least had lived a life. In an attempt to somehow cheer you up, people might send you gifts, things that seem inappropriate at such a time, they might invite you to do things that seem ridiculous or they might turn up at your house expecting to be able to spend time with you when all you want to do is hide yourself away.

It is almost inevitable that someone will say or do something that jars and makes you wish they had opted not to say anything at all. They say and do these things not because they are bad people, but because your grief makes them uncomfortable. With the death of a child, we are all reminded of the cruelty and chaos of the world we live in, and, for many people, that is an unbearable truth. They want to make you feel better, because, if you are OK, maybe that truth won't be so true.

It is important to remember that if someone seems to avoid you, or if they say something very insensitive or do something that feels thoughtless and hurtful, the intention is usually well-meant and the person is more than likely ill-equipped to deal with the enormity of your loss. The world is a grief-illiterate place and few of us have been shown how to offer support to someone who is grieving for their child. If it is possible to focus on the well-meant intention behind the funny card or the insensitive invitation to a party, or even to understand the silence they keep, that can make a seemingly insensitive person seem less so.

A couple who were offered a meeting to hear the details of their child's medical condition and subsequent death with a very nervous young doctor told me afterwards: 'He was utterly useless, Jenni. He said all the wrong things. But we knew he cared. And that made it all right.' Or, to put it another way: it's not what they say, it's how they say it that counts.

If you are supporting someone whose child has died: Some suggestions

'Grief is about witnessing, not fixing.'

David Kessler, *Grief.com*

- Bereaved parents may not want you to feel sorry for them. But being empathic with them – that is, wanting to understand, but also being far enough removed from their painful feelings – can be comforting because it provides a safe enough environment for their grief, which at times can feel overwhelming and frightening to them. Being empathic with a friend or relative who is grieving for a child can mean simply listening while they share, without offering any advice or judgement. Simply being there in silence can sometimes be enough.

- Ask bereaved parents about their child and try not to ignore what has happened. Many parents love to hear their child's name and to be able to talk about them. Ask to see photographs and show an interest. Parents

---

don't stop wanting to talk about their child simply because they have died. Our children are as important to us after they have died as when they were alive.

- While a sensitive suggestion to go for a walk or see a film may be appropriate at the right time, bear in mind that no one can ever truly mend a grieving parent's broken heart. Their child has died, and there is nothing to do but be there for them if and when they would like you to be. Simply by being there you are doing the best for them that you can.

- Practical help with whatever is right for them, such as offering to do some shopping or clearing snow from a drive in bad weather, can mean as much to grieving parents as any grand gestures. Knowing there is no pressure from you to acknowledge your help or spend time with you makes these gestures even more meaningful.

- Important dates and milestones can be especially difficult for parents – not only birthdays and cultural or religious holidays such as Christmas, but unexpected occasions like exam results day, the back-to-school period or even the weddings of their children's friends. Just remembering with a simple note or message to say you are thinking about them and here to help if they need you can be very comforting.

- It is never too late to tell people how sad you are to hear the news about their child's death. After one of her twin sons, Nicky, was killed in an IRA bomb attack, his mother, Countess Mountbatten of Burma, told me how she found great comfort in the messages and cards she received from strangers all over the world for many years after his death.

Understanding grief and how it may affect us will help you face the challenges it brings every day. But bereaved parents have shown me that every parent's grief is as unique, complex and surprising as the child they are mourning. It will grow and change, and will require a great deal of your care and attention throughout your life. And, in time, it may be something you can take into your heart and carry with you.

Chapter 2

The Different Circumstances of a Child's Death

'And can it be that in a world so full and busy, the loss of one weak creature makes a void in any heart, so wide and deep that nothing but the width and depth of vast eternity can fill it up!'

Charles Dickens, *Dombey and Son*

It is important to acknowledge that the way your child dies can impact the way you experience grief. When a child's death is sudden, parents have no time to prepare mentally or emotionally for what has happened. The sense of loss is complicated by the accompanying shock and disbelief. When a child's death has been expected, perhaps after an illness or a terminal diagnosis, the grief felt by parents is no less painful. Parents who know their child will die face the reality of that forthcoming death every day, week or month until it happens. And, when it finally does, there is still an enormous amount of shock and disbelief. However a child dies, it will always be the worst thing that can happen for any parent.

We will explore how grief for your child may feel different at different ages in later chapters, but there is a point that is important to make here and it is something I will refer to repeatedly in this book. The love and deep attachment a parent feels for their child is the same regardless of age, whether their child is alive or dead, a newborn baby or a 21-year-old familiar with adult responsibilities about to embark on adulthood. This is especially true for biological mothers, whose blood and tissue remain physically intertwined with their child's for years, sometimes decades, after a child is born. This is called 'maternal fetal chimerism'. A biological mother's cells can remain part of her child's cellular make-up for many years, so that a mother and child are not simply close relations, they are cellular extensions of one another – and it is no exaggeration to say that, when her child dies, a part of a mother dies, too. It is natural to feel such a great loss.

The unique nature of the biological maternal bond does not ever diminish the grief felt by biological fathers, who are so often expected to be strong and stoic in this experience and have historically been encouraged by medical professionals not to dwell or linger on the matter. Nor does it diminish the enormous shock and lifetime of complicated feelings and sadness felt by the siblings of the dead child. Grandparents, uncles and aunts, step-parents and other close family and friends all experience the death of a loved child in their own ways – their families have been forever altered and relationships within them are now highly likely to struggle and strain under the enormous pressure of grief. Adoptive parents and those families who have had a child through surrogacy or other methods of fertility treatment also face a terrible version of grief. These families have often been through enormous struggles to have the child who they must now live without again. However a family is configured and however a child has died, no death is worse than another. There is no hierarchy, only difference. We will explore family relationships and dynamics in grief in Chapters 6 and 7 (pages 116 and 133).

When Their Death Is an Accident

Children of all ages can die unexpectedly for many reasons, but accidents are one of the biggest causes. Watching our children explore and learn is a great pleasure of parenting at any age. As parents, we know instinctively that children of all ages need to experience certain levels of risk and independence so that they can learn to manage danger, understand their limits and become familiar with their instincts. But sometimes, when a child of any age is curious or brave enough and the circumstances do not favour their well-intentioned investigations, tragic and fatal accidents can and do happen.

Falling, drowning, road accidents, poisoning via medicines, suffocation, strangulation, choking, fire-related accidents, pranks gone wrong and drug overdoses can all cause the deaths of children and young people. Adult children are also exposed to the dangers and difficulties of being independent, just as all of us are. It is never possible to protect our children, whatever their age, from the very many ways in which some children can die by accident.

However an accidental and unforeseen death occurs, it can make it incredibly difficult for parents to accept the cause of their child's death. The pure unnecessariness of it, the waste of a child's life when all that they had been engaged in was normal behaviour and very often fun and play, can seem especially cruel – a stark and unwanted reminder of the world's ruthlessness and the place we occupy in it. This sense of injustice adds another layer to the grief experienced by parents whose child has died in an accident.

If this is you, the unbearably hard work of accepting your child's death might be doubled by the frustration you feel and the need to accept such difficult circumstances.

Sudden Unexplained Death

Children can also die unexpectedly and with no reason without it being an accident or a medical condition. Sudden unexplained death in childhood (SUDC) and, if the child is a baby, sudden infant death syndrome (SIDS) are both terms for when the cause of death is unexplainable and happens without forewarning. This often, although not exclusively, happens when the child is asleep. A child, and sometimes an adult child, can go to bed entirely healthy and happy and simply never wake up again. Sometimes an undiagnosed condition is discovered, but sometimes a death like this is something that cannot ever be accounted for with scientific evidence or reason. While no child's death is any more or less senseless than another, the agonising mystery of an unexplained death adds another layer to the burden carried by the parents of the dead child. Having nothing to pin their child's death on, no disease or accident or another person to blame can make an already unbearable reality feel not only illogical, but almost malevolent in its refusal to bear the fruit of a clear explanation. Many parents in this situation feel a sense of confusion and restlessness and a lack of understanding from the world around them.

Their pain is often amplified by the fact that the sudden death of a child is treated by the authorities as suspicious and, in most cases, parents must immediately be interviewed by the police and their child's death becomes a coroner's case. Their child's body must be taken away or, if they have taken the child into hospital, parents must go home without the child they arrived with. They are not allowed to touch or cuddle or hold their child's body as investigators do not want to disturb possible forensic evidence. And they have very little control over what happens next, sometimes for weeks and even months, as investigations are carried out and verdicts reached.

If your child died unexpectedly and with no reason, because this kind of death is so traumatic, it is very hard to talk about and for other people to help you. There is such a great deal that is unknown, and this can create a kind of grief cul-de-sac that at times feels like it cannot ever be exited. Friends don't know what to say, professionals often aren't trained enough or given the time in this situation and there is simply not enough support for bereaved families or professionals going through this trauma.

The charity SUDC UK was set up by Nikki and Tom Speed in 2019, whose healthy two-year-old daughter, Rosie, died unexpectedly and without explanation. As well as pioneering medical research in the field, SUDC UK offers support and guidance if you are experiencing this specific kind of death of a child. There is more about Nikki's experience in Chapters 4 and 7 (pages 85 and 136) and on SUDC UK in Chapter 8 (page 166).

On Traumatic Grief

In his bestselling book *The Body Keeps the Score*, Bessel van der Kolk writes of trauma:

> 'We have learned that trauma is not just an event that took place sometime in the past; it is also the imprint left by that experience on mind, brain, and body. This imprint has ongoing consequences for how the human organism manages to survive in the

present. Trauma results in a fundamental reorganization of the way the mind and brain manage perceptions. It changes not only how we think and what we think about, but also our very capacity to think.'

For all parents, the loss of a child feels traumatic. It is perhaps the most traumatic event any parent will ever experience. However, for some, if their baby or child's death has been a complete shock and happened under especially difficult or distressing circumstances, and especially if the parent has been present or witnessed the death, it can create what is recognised as a trauma reaction.

A parent who has experienced a traumatic event around the death of their child may find it hard to talk about it in a natural way, because it is just too frightening to say what has happened. Instead of a parent being able to remember and talk about the story of their child's death to a friend or loved one, they may bury the pain of the event that caused the death because it is too horrifying for them to speak about. This means that sometimes external events can trigger this grief which lies stored, causing an involuntary reaction. It could be the feel of a certain fabric, the smell of alcohol or the sound of an ambulance; almost anything that might be associated with the trauma of their child's death can become triggering for an affected parent and provoke vivid flashbacks, extreme panic and paralysing distress. A parent experiencing the recurring distressing images and vivid flashbacks of traumatic grief might appear to completely freeze and be unable to talk or move, or sweat and be sick, and be in a kind of shock. The effects of this recurring state can inhibit a parent's ability to fully grieve, cry and feel the necessary and natural sadness about what has happened. It is different for everyone who has it – the only common factor is the sense of overwhelming fear, anxiety and paralysis experienced by a parent in a traumatic reaction.

If you feel that you may have this kind of extreme anxiety around the circumstances of your child's death, if talking about it feels almost impossible and certain triggers affect your ability to function, then it is important that you find an appropriately qualified counsellor (see page 51 for advice on this). It is only by talking about the events of your child's death and acknowledging the trauma you have experienced that you can begin to grieve. Eye movement desensitisation and reprocessing (EMDR) is a psychotherapy technique that can help people recover from distressing experiences and has been very successful for many of the parents I have supported. It can never change the events that have happened, but by a simple process of repetition and verbalising the pain, it can make it more 'real' and, in doing so, allow you to talk about it more openly. Look for a counsellor who is trained in EMDR and trauma counselling. The work of the clinical psychologist David Trickey may also be useful to parents and siblings experiencing traumatic grief. His website and the details of the UK Trauma Council can also be found on pages 173 and 176.

When a Child is Murdered

It is an impermissible truth that children can sometimes die at the hands of someone else. Sometimes a child is murdered by those who know them well, such as relatives or caregivers, sometimes by a stranger. Circumstances are unique to every death caused by murder, but themes of abuse, faith, revenge, substance abuse, long-term illness, gang culture, terrorism and psychiatric problems can be intrinsic when a child dies at the hands of someone else, either an adult or another child.

If a child has been killed by someone close to them, and to the parents, the enormity of their death is amplified by the knowledge that someone they knew has caused it. While there is evidently someone to blame for a child's death in this situation, there is also very often so much that parents cannot ever know.

There is also a torrent of justly felt anger and blame, for the person who killed their child, sometimes for themselves and nearly always for the world in which we live, that could let such a terrible thing happen.

A mother was accused of murdering her two-year-old daughter, who died while at nursery. The staff at the nursery insisted that the girl had arrived that day with symptoms of illness and the mother had deliberately left her there when she was unwell. However, the mother protested her innocence and was eventually proven to be innocent when the post-mortem revealed her daughter had been badly shaken and hurt, and that her injuries suggested this had happened at a time when she was in the care of the nursery. The vindication her mother felt was welcome, but paled in significance to the anger and agony of not knowing what or how her little girl had felt in the moments before her death.

If your child has died by murder, police family liaison officers can be extremely important. They are highly trained and sensitive professionals who can act as a link between you and the investigation teams after a child has been murdered.

Sandra, whose daughter Lucy, 30, was killed in the Bali nightclub bombing of 2002, describes how their family liaison officer helped her and her husband, Bob:

> 'We first met our family liaison officer, Colin, when he turned up on our doorstep, along with his Detective Sergeant, two days after Lucy was murdered in the bombings. Needless to say, we were in extreme shock and felt numb after the news that our precious Lucy had been killed. Colin stayed by our side and helped us through the horror and officialdom of the weeks that followed. He completed all the necessary forms, accompanied us to Lucy's flat to collect DNA, briefed us on publicity, liaised with the travel company that took Lucy to Bali, sorted out her travel insurance and

finances, and accompanied us to Lucy's place of work. He also attended meetings we arranged with the Foreign & Commonwealth Office and came with us to the regular meetings of a group we formed for the 28 British people who died that day and the survivors. We were already so grateful to him for his support and guidance, but the best was yet to come.

'We flew to Bali where Colin met us to help us try to locate our daughter. He arranged all the travel details and booked us into the same hotel Lucy had been staying at and arranged it so that we could see her room. He also arranged for us to visit the site where she died, and we laid wreaths at various memorials and met dignitaries, always under the strictest of security arrangements. At the same time, he was working on recovering the jewellery our daughter was wearing at the time she died. After four difficult days in Bali, we were able to return to the UK with the jewellery Lucy was wearing on the night of the bombing – such treasured possessions. What Colin did for us was so amazing that we nominated him for an MBE and it was a very special moment for us when he went to the Palace to collect his award.'

After a Child's Suicide

While every child's death is deeply painful, suicide brings with it a unique cohort of pain for bereaved parents. Not only has your child died, but they have decided to do so. It is entirely normal to feel deeply rejected by your child and to feel that you have failed or not been a good enough parent to them. It is also common to blame yourself for not having known they were thinking about suicide and for not having been able to stop them. It can take many years for the parents of children who have taken their own lives to come to terms with the facts of their child's death and to find any kind of peace of mind about the way things happened and the circumstances which may or may not have led to their actions.

To make things harder, there is always a public inquiry or an inquest after a suicide, and this means that the details of your child's death can be freely reported by the media. Media reporting of suicide is far more sensitive now than ever and there is greater awareness of the importance of language (for example, we no longer talk about suicide being 'committed' since it is no longer considered to be a crime), the dangers of glamorising suicide and the phenomenon of suicide contagion. But insensitive, inappropriate language and a scandalising tone to the way these deaths are reported still pervade and sadly do nothing to help the parents who are grieving the loss of their precious child. Parents of children who have ended their own lives can feel the harsh judgement of society at large, and the pressure of speculation among family, friends and strangers about what happened and why your child decided to do what they did.

In addition to the pain of feeling so rejected and judged, as well as the natural devastating grief every parent feels for their child, many parents cannot ever truly know why their child ended their life or how they were feeling at the end. Suicides are never the same, like the people whose lives they claim, and the impact of every death by suicide varies according to many factors: whether it has been anticipated; how it is carried out and the impact of this on their body and other people; whether a child chooses to leave a message or letter to explain their reasons to their parents; how and by whom their body is found; and the level of investigation following their death. It is not by its nature something anyone can ever know how to manage and many parents feel they are stumbling through the days, weeks, months and years that follow their child's suicide.

If your child has ended their life, the support of a counsellor (see page 51) and/or a support group will almost certainly be very helpful. There is more about grief following a suicide in Chapter 5 (page 107) and details of organisations that can help on page 172.

When a Child's Death Is Anticipated

For some parents, the knowledge that the child they love will die before them is something they have lived with for some time. Whether a child has a terminal illness or was born with a life-limiting disability, parents in this position must live with and manage the spectre of their grief even while their child is alive.

As Nic, mum of Naomi who was born with a rare genetic condition and died aged seven, writes: 'The distress caused by a diagnosis like this is impossible to describe. My grief for Naomi began at her birth and was acknowledged finally at the point of her diagnosis. Despite the fact that we knew her condition was incurable, the grief when she actually died was overwhelming.'

Many parents describe sensing that those around them expect them to feel a kind of relief when their child dies, to be unburdened of their suffering once they have gone. In my experience of working with the parents of children who have died after a long illness or life-shortening disability, nothing could be further from the truth. Their children's lives have not been a burden but a joy. As Nic writes:

> 'In between her diagnosis and death, her life and ours became full of joy. Led by her, we scaled down our lives to appreciate the very small things – the smiles that she brought to us, the tenderness that she evoked in others, her laugh, her love of her pets, her love of fresh air and camping. She was a cherished member of her school and was loved at her hospice. Her happiness at the birth of her

brother, Hamish, born free of the condition, and
our two years together as a family of four, was the
happiest time of our lives. Despite the challenges,
we learned to live moment to moment and, in a
strange way, our lives grew from small to big.'

The death of a poorly child can also leave a very large void
where caring for them once took place. Illness, with all its
hospital visits and treatments and consultations, creates just
as much busy-ness and occupies as much time as parenting a
healthy child, and so the sudden sense of being without the
core focus of a child to care for hits parents in this situation
every bit as hard as a sudden or unexpected death. Although it
has been on the horizon for some time, parents of a child with
a long-term illness who has died can find they have been so
focused on caring for their child and, in some cases, so full of
hope that they might recover, that their death is not something
they have prepared for at all.

Writes Nic:

'When Naomi died, the grief for her felt bottomless.
Not only the loss of her sunny, kind presence and
the tenderness she brought out in others, but the
disappearance from our lives of her incredible
carers, who had grown as close as family; her
school teachers, doctors and nurses, hospice team,
play specialists, friends, even the loss of regular
medical appointments and the devoted specialists
who were so dedicated to giving her the best quality
of life with her rare condition. All of this left us
bereft in so many unfathomable and unimaginable
ways.'

What to expect when a child dies in hospital

If you are reading this in the knowledge that your child will soon die in hospital or a hospice, it be might helpful for you to know a little about what to expect. Hopefully, you will already have had the sensitive care and support of your child's care team and you will be well-informed about what happens once your child has died. This will be especially true if your child has received or is receiving palliative care in a hospice; they will have been under the compassionate care of expert hospice staff and you will hopefully have been well supported and informed about what happens when your child dies. But sometimes in a hospital setting things can happen very quickly and you may not be able to take in all the information or keep track of fast-moving events.

The important thing to know is that you can and will have as much time as you need with your child after they have died. You can also be reassured that after their death their body will be carefully and respectfully placed either in a cool cot or bed, or in the hospital mortuary until you are ready for them to be taken to the funeral home.

In the moments after they die, if your child has been attached to any machinery, all tubes and monitors can now be turned off and removed, and you will be able to hold and cuddle your child for as long as you wish to. You can also choose to wash and dress your child with or without the help of a nurse, should you wish to. Many parents find it very comforting to dress their child or baby in their clothes from home or a favourite outfit. Some parents want to take photographs, especially if their child is a baby. You may also wish to have your child's body blessed, even if you are not religious, and you can ask your nurse to help you contact your hospital's faith representative and arrange this. If you are considering donating any of your child's organs, a specialist nurse for organ donation will talk to you before your child dies about what happens.

After a while, your child's body will be taken to the hospital mortuary where you can also arrange to spend time with them again in a separate room if you wish to. Some parents find this comforting; others find it very difficult to see their child like this as their body will be extremely cold. Some choose to read stories and bring a soft toy to their young children. Hospital morticians are highly experienced and professional people who will understand your need to see your child and make the experience as discreet and comfortable for you as they can.

All deaths must be legally registered within five days by the Registrar in the district where your child has died, and a funeral cannot take place until this has happened. If there is no need for a post-mortem, your child's body can be collected, either by you or by the funeral director if you are using one, as soon as you are ready. If there is a need for a post-mortem, your child's body may need to stay at the mortuary until that has been completed.

Although anticipated, the death of a child is always an enormous shock and, if you are grieving a child in this way, you need every bit as much support and care from those around you as those experiencing a sudden or traumatic grief.

Nic went on to found an award-winning charity called SLOW (Surviving the Loss of Your World), to help provide counselling and support to other bereaved parents, and there is more about this in Chapter 8 (page 167).

Finding a Bereavement Counsellor

You may wish to seek the support of a bereavement counsellor after your child has died. Having the time and space to talk about your child and your feelings about their death with someone neutral is almost always very helpful; not because a counsellor can ever say anything that will make you feel better or give you advice about how you should live now that your child has died, but because they are trained professionals who can gently help you make sense of your feelings and encourage you to reflect on issues or worries that might be impacting you and your relationships. Counselling sessions are also a safe place to confidentially explore and offload thoughts and feelings you might be unable to express to others comfortably. Some parents find support like this very helpful and continue to see their counsellors for many years, sometimes along with their partners and other children. But how do you find the right counsellor for you and what should you be looking for in a grief counsellor?

Where to find a bereavement counsellor

Often, bereavement counsellors are recommended by friends and through word of mouth, and this can be a very good way to find someone, especially if they are recommended by someone you know and trust. Some charities, especially those that are related to your child's cause of death, can provide bereavement counselling that is either partially or fully funded, though you may need to apply and/or wait a while for their services to be available. If you are looking for a private grief counsellor, it is always best to find a registered therapist via the British Association for Counselling and Psychotherapy (BACP – see page 172 for details). Many local authorities also offer bereavement services and it is worth checking your local council's website for support groups and services that are local to you. While they usually can't address your individual concerns in detail, groups can be a wonderful way to share your feelings and meet other parents who are experiencing grief for their child.

How to choose a bereavement counsellor

The directory of counsellors in the UK is enormous and knowing which one to choose is very hard. Some useful questions and considerations when choosing a potential counsellor include:

- *How much bereavement training and other relevant counselling experience does the person have?* Experience isn't the only thing that matters, but choosing someone who is familiar and comfortable with the specific nature of grief counselling and, ideally, who has trained in this area, can make a real difference to your experience. If your child's death has involved a traumatic loss and you are experiencing flashbacks and other difficulties associated with this, then a counsellor who is trained in trauma and techniques such as EMDR will also be very helpful.

- *Can the counsellor see you as a couple?* Partners often find they manage their grief very differently. Attending counselling as a couple can help you both feel seen and heard and help you to understand each other. There is more on managing the parent relationship in Chapter 6 (page 117).

- *Would your sessions be in person or online?* We are all more accustomed to online meetings nowadays, but not everyone feels comfortable talking to a screen. Some people like to go somewhere away from home to talk about grief, while others feel safer in familiar surroundings. Establish how your potential counsellor will work and think about what is right for you.

- *How does the chemistry between you and your potential counsellor feel?* A good counsellor will ideally offer you a short initial session at no charge, to meet and establish whether you both feel you are a good fit for each other. They will want to do this for themselves as much as for you.

The American psychologist and founder of client-centred therapy Carl Rogers identified three core elements that should be present in a successful client/counsellor relationship. They are:

1. Unconditional positive regard: The therapist needs to accept the client for who they are, no matter what they say or do.

2. Empathy: The therapist must understand and respect the client's perspective.

3. Congruence: The therapist is authentic and allows their true personality to come through.

You don't need to scrutinise your potential counsellor for evidence of these concepts, but paying attention to the way you feel in your counsellor's presence is generally a very good idea. Try to notice if you are comfortable and able to be yourself, and ask yourself if you feel they are also being authentic. Congruence – the idea that we are our true selves with one another – is the basis of all successful counsellor and client relationships.

- *How many sessions will you have and how much will they cost?* All counsellors have different approaches, so it is worth understanding what kind of framework you can expect to work with. Some like to run a set number of sessions while others are more fluid. Some counsellors charge very high fees and others are more realistic. Unfortunately, you will need to pay for your sessions, so it is important to establish what the costs will be for you going forward. Charities and trusts such as the Amy Robinson Foundation and Teddy's Wish (see pages 166 and 168 for details) can sometimes help provide grief counselling, so please do not give up on the idea if money is an issue.

Planning Your Child's Funeral or Memorial Service

Many parents choose to use the services of a funeral director when their child dies. Funeral directors are highly trained and professional people who can guide you sensitively through the process of moving your child's body, keeping them in a safe and appropriate place, arranging burial plots and cremation, choosing a coffin and arranging a service – whether religious or non-religious. When you are almost certainly likely to be in a state of shock, knowing that someone else is taking care of the details can be reassuring. Most funeral directors will be able to offer you a range of contacts and services so that you can create an occasion that feels personal and meaningful to you.

However, it is worth knowing that using the services of a funeral director is not a legal requirement in the UK and you can choose to organise your child's funeral yourself if you wish to. You can keep your child's body at home until the funeral and move your child's body by your own means of transport. If they are being buried, you can dig their grave and choose to bury them in a number of locations other than churchyards and burial grounds, including on private land such as a garden. However, there are a number of very important laws and restrictions around these choices, and you will need to contact your local authority for guidance on seeking the relevant permissions. Some local councils run their own funeral services, especially for people who do not want a faith-based funeral for their child.

Some parents choose to hold a religious ceremony within their local faith community and this can be very reassuring and familiar, especially if your family is actively involved in the community. However, a funeral does not need to be a religious ceremony or follow a traditional format. The bereaved parents I have supported have chosen to do some wonderful things to say goodbye to their child in their own way, from an a cappella choir in the church to a day of celebration for their child's life at their family home. There is no correct way to hold a funeral for your child; only the way that feels right for you.

Your child's funeral: Some things you might find useful

Funerals can be expensive and the death of a child is not something anyone expects to need to pay for. Many funeral directors do not charge fees for the funeral of a baby or child; however, there can be additional costs, such as hiring vehicles, buying burial plots or paying for cremation services. The good news is that there is plenty of help available if the costs are a worry. The Children's Funeral Fund for England, the Funeral Support Payment in Scotland and the Child Funeral Fund in Northern Ireland can all offer help with funeral costs, and, in Wales, you can apply to have your costs reimbursed. If you are using one, a funeral director can usually assist you in applying for this help. The Citizen's Advice Bureau (see page 172) will also be able to tell you about the help available to you locally. All the current information is available online at GOV.UK.

If you are arranging the funeral yourself, your local council will be able to help you with the information you need about burial plots, crematorium services and support with costs. Humanists UK and the Institute of Civil Funerals can also help with advice on non-religious funerals. Details of both are on page 174.

If you are using a funeral director, check they are registered with either the National Association of Funeral Directors (NAFD) or the National Society of Allied and Independent Funeral Directors (SAIF), as these are the two main professional bodies.

Siblings and other children in the family can feel a range of complex emotions on the day of their sibling's funeral – from envy and resentment to isolation and a sense of helplessness. You may find it helpful to ask your child or children if they would like to take on certain roles during the day, whether it is handing out the Orders of Service or reading something out. Being an important part of the proceedings helps to create positive memories for them of the day. There is more on this and on siblings in grief in Chapter 7 (page 133).

However your child dies it will alter forever your experience as a parent, and send ripples of grief through your own life and those of your other children and family members. To know and accept that your child has died is one of the greatest challenges any human being can ever be asked to face. Know that simply by being here, reading these words, you have already come so far and, in the worst circumstances life can offer, you are doing the very best you can.

Chapter 3

When a Baby Dies

'I would have loved my baby so – and cared for it so tenderly – and tried to give her every chance for good. And yet I wasn't allowed to keep her.'

L. M. Montgomery, *Anne of Green Gables*

The grief a parent feels for a baby who has died is grief for someone who may have had the chance to live only for a few minutes, hours, days or months. Yet, this precious child will have been loved as fiercely and profoundly as if they had lived a full life. When a baby dies, parents who have been anticipating the greatest love and joy of their lives now find themselves in profound shock, grieving for everything they had hoped for and never had the chance to know about their child. The start of a new life and everything they longed for has ended in such tragedy.

Along with the elderly, babies are human beings at their most vulnerable and therefore most susceptible to fatality. Many more babies die before, at, or in the weeks and months after birth than older children. There are many reasons why they can die. Sometimes there is a problem during the later stages of pregnancy and a baby dies inside its mother's womb and she must then give birth to her stillborn baby. Sometimes there are complications and a baby dies during labour and this is also called a stillbirth. Sometimes a baby dies in the first few hours and weeks of life. When a baby dies later on, after they have been taken home, it can be because of an illness, an accident or SIDS, where nobody can explain the death of a baby in medical terms; it simply happens and there is no known reason found at the legally required post-mortem. If a pregnancy ends before 24 weeks of gestation, this is called a miscarriage, and if it is before 13 weeks this is called an early miscarriage. In reality, though, there is never a clearly defined distinction, and many women who experience a miscarriage, especially at a late stage, feel the same grief and despair as someone who has experienced what is termed a stillbirth. Ultimately, these labels are more useful for medical professionals than their patients and language should not affect your feelings or imply that your loss is somehow greater or less than.

The memories of the time parents have with their baby are incredibly precious. They might only be for the length of a pregnancy, sometimes the birth and, if their baby has lived for a few hours or a few months, the short time they have had with them. However long their baby has lived for, these memories will be all they have to last a lifetime. The sheer scarcity of time parents have had with their baby and the need to hold on to the memories of them is what makes the grief felt for a baby so deep and painful. For some people, it is the only pregnancy and the only baby they will ever have.

'It was a devastating, lonely, distressing and frightening experience and I struggled to pick up the threads of my life,' says Celine, a mother who went into labour in mid-pregnancy and whose son, James, died before he was delivered.

Although not always the case, a baby has usually been longed for and their families are most often extraordinarily excited about their arrival. Their lives have been consumed with looking forward to and planning for their baby's birth; such a vast amount of love, nurture and anticipation goes into any pregnancy. Western medicine tells us more than ever about our babies as they grow inside us. We can hear their heartbeats and may choose to know their genders, so that the process of getting to know and form an attachment to our babies begins far sooner for their waiting parents than ever before. Although it can also be full of trepidation and illness, for many women and their partners, pregnancy is the most wonderful thing that has happened. A baby is never simply a baby – they are the representation of a union between two people, a woman's journey to motherhood and a family's ancestral heritage. Babies are about hope and new beginnings, purpose and joy, and almost always the best of human intentions.

Death Before, At or Soon After Birth

Some parents may know before the birth that their baby has died. At whatever stage in her pregnancy it happens, it is often the case that an expectant mother notices her baby hasn't moved in the usual way for some time and medical checks reveal what she has already feared: that the baby's heartbeat has stopped. Because there is no heartbeat to record, the midwife will know that your baby is not alive and will need a medical colleague to confirm the death. Waiting for this terrible news is truly heart-breaking and can create complicated feelings of panic as well as sadness and grief. Humans are programmed to fear death in all its forms, so to know that a death has taken place inside you is an unbearable reality. The baby you love so much is not going to have a life.

Some women in this situation choose to be immediately induced into labour for a vaginal delivery, and some may need to be induced for medical reasons. Others choose to go home and come back later when they feel ready to give birth. This means parents can bring back some clothes for their baby to wear when they are born and many have told me how pleased they are that they did this, even if it was for that one and only time. Caesarean sections are rarely offered as they are not considered to be medically necessary in these circumstances.

Sometimes, when there are complications before the birth, a mother must make truly harrowing decisions about her baby's life and their death, before they are even born. If a serious condition or abnormality is discovered, or if her own life is at risk, she may need to go through a termination for medical reasons – this can happen up to full term if necessary – and she may then need to give birth to the baby. Some parents choose to continue with the pregnancy knowing their child will die shortly after their birth, as ending their life beforehand is not something they feel able to do. There is no right decision for parents to make in these circumstances and parents who experience this kind of loss need as much careful and compassionate support as other parents. For more information and valuable support, the charity Antenatal Results & Choices (ARC – see page 172) can be exceptionally helpful and understanding. See also GOV.UK and the other resources on pages 172–178.

Going through labour and giving birth to a baby who has died can be a frightening experience that remains etched on a mother's mind forever. A midwife will always guide and support a mother though this, and mothers can expect to receive more pain relief that usual since there is no concern about harming the baby. Not only does a mother experience much of the usual pain and physical exhaustion associated with childbirth, but she must somehow try to make sense of the confusing reality she is now faced with. To be told that your baby has not survived, that you are no longer required to nourish and protect the child you have grown inside you, is devastating news. Your body has been primed for your baby's arrival, so much energy has gone into preparations and now it has nowhere to go. Your baby has died, yet you are still a new mother.

In the case of a multiple pregnancy, sometimes a mum must make the decision whether to terminate one of her pregnancies if the baby is not compatible with life.

During a routine 20-week scan, a mum who was expecting twins was told that one of her babies, the girl who she had named Zoe, was developing normally and the other, a boy who she had named Alex, had a condition that was not compatible with life. The condition, known as anencephaly, meant he would be born without parts of his brain and skull, and would not be able to live outside of the womb. His mother was offered an injection to terminate the pregnancy of her son (a procedure known as selective foeticide), but she chose to continue with her twin pregnancy. She was very clear that she wanted both of her unborn babies to have the same experience and treatment by doctors. Both babies were born by natural birth and her son lived for about three hours. She was able to register his birth and put them both in a cot together where she took photographs. She told me how proud she felt of them both and that she had been able to see and hold her son before he had died.

However it happens, when a baby dies before or around their birth, a mother's body will then also go through the many physical changes and stages that happen afterwards. Her breasts will produce milk as though her baby had lived, and she may face many days and weeks of physical pain, bleeding and fluctuating hormones while her body heals. Parents have told me that this time can feel like an emotional and physical black hole. It is never easy to experience or recover from; it can seem like nature is playing a cruel joke.

If you are experiencing these feelings, don't be afraid to ask for support from those around you. There is pain relief and other medication to help with some of the difficult physical symptoms, such as milk coming in, and you can expect good care and support from your midwives and other medical professionals who are trained to help and will be aware of how difficult this process is for you.

Knowing how to be with your stillborn baby

For many, concentrating on getting through the delivery of their baby who has died is paramount. It is only after the baby has been delivered that parents are able to consider the thought of seeing their dead baby. This can be a shocking and even frightening experience for some, while for others it can feel like the most natural thing in the world. Hopefully, you have had sensitive care from a midwife and a team who are aware of how important this time is for you and the impact it will have on your feelings in the future.

It is natural when a new baby dies for mothers to not know how to be when seeing their baby for the first time. If you are helped soon after your birth to gradually consider the importance of seeing your baby in their completeness and holding them, this can be extremely comforting. Parents have taught me that they need to be gently supported when seeing and holding their dead baby for the first time. Being helped to hold and examine their tiny features, despite any physical problems they may have, can be a huge comfort to parents at this time and in the future.

A neonatal death after birth

Sometimes a baby is born prematurely or with a condition that means they will need to stay in hospital for specialist care after they are born. When this happens, new parents have to leave their baby in hospital and go home with empty arms. They then live in a state of painful limbo, going back and forth to the hospital SCBU or the neonatal intensive care unit (NICU) to see their babies and be as close to them as they can before having to leave them again. Staff on these hospital units are trained in parents' emotional needs and are always helpful and supportive at what is an exhausting time for parents, who are overwhelmed with uncertainties: not knowing how or if their baby will get better and waiting for test results, when all they want to do is take their precious new baby home and be able to bond with them.

The time I spent with psychologist and psychiatrist John Bowlby taught me why the drive for both baby and mother to stay close and form these early bonds is very strong. The setting of a hospital special care unit can be an extremely challenging environment for this natural instinct and for parents who are usually desperate to hold their baby and care for them free from machinery and away from the clinical hospital space. When their baby dies, it is usually after a period of such hope and desperation that this death feels especially cruel.

Baby Jason was born with a condition called achondroplasia. He had a perfect little face and lots of dark hair. He needed oxygen support to breathe as his rib cage was compromised and he lived for 11 days. His mum described what a relief it was to finally be able to hold him as he died peacefully in her arms and to have time with him alone, away from the machines and other people, shortly afterwards:

> 'I asked them to take out his feeding tube which they did and then I stood up and carried him to my room. It was incredible! This was the first

time I had been able to carry my baby anywhere without the tubes, the oxygen, the worry that it would be bad for him. The freedom of carrying and cuddling my baby like this for the first time! He was still warm; he could have been alive, just asleep. I wanted to walk off with him, carry him away with me off into the blue.'

However brief the time parents spend with their baby in this situation, it can be extremely intense as such great hope and love are mixed up with sadness and loss. Caren, whose twin son Jacques died on the NICU after seven days, described her sense of helplessness:

'I was filled with love and optimism in the NICU. I had become a mother to not one, but two magical souls; it felt like destiny and the care and positivity from the staff in the seven days we were on the unit just intensified my excitement for the future.

'Tragically, it all changed overnight and Jacques died. He was a week old. We were with him when his tiny heart could not cope, watching hopelessly as the doctors and nurses tried to save our son and keep our family together. That was the first time in my life I felt truly helpless, and it was impossible to me that Ben and I could do nothing to save our son – we were mere spectators in that moment. They took away all the tubes and wires and brought Jacques to us in the room we had called home for seven days. And, together with his twin brother Xavier, we spent time holding him, talking to him and showering him with kisses and love. He was perfect; just a warm, sleeping baby.

'The pain was excruciating, pure physical agony. Loss is so consuming, uncontrollable and frightening at times. I needed to wrap myself in the

love of my husband and my lone beautiful baby
boy who was missing his whole other half. Would
Xavier be okay alone?'

Becoming a mother and losing a child at the same time is
certainly complicated. As Caren says, for those with twins or
triplets, the experience can become even more emotionally
complex. Suzie, a mum of twin sons Rory, who was stillborn
at 24 weeks, and Daniel, who died 5 weeks later, 18 hours after
being born, went on to set up a charity, Footprints Baby Loss,
especially for the bereaved parents of multiple pregnancies and
births (see pages 168 and 173 for details). She says:

> 'When there is a death within twins or triplets,
> there are always more variables because there is
> more than one baby to consider and, for every
> medical issue and treatment, both babies need to
> be considered. Because of this, it also means that
> there are many different scenarios for how a baby
> or babies in a twin or triplet pregnancy can die. It
> is often highly complex, traumatic and prolonged.
> It can make the grief complex too.'

Another mum, Sharon, who co-founded Footprints Baby Loss
with Suzie, explains how, after her twins Charlie and Joshua
were born prematurely and lived for seven and thirteen days
respectively, the support from other parents who had experienced similar deaths was invaluable: 'It was such a relief to talk
to somebody else who had a similar experience to myself, and I
felt so much less alone. I am really proud to be a twin mum and
I still love to talk about Charlie and Joshua.'

The lack of memories and time you have with your baby
or babies is one of the greatest challenges when they die. If
you are able to, take as many photographs of your baby as
you can. You don't have to look at them straight away – you
can decide whether to look at them at any stage and you won't

later regret having nothing to see or to help you believe what has happened. You may have been able to wash and dress your baby, and you can take photographs of this as well. As frightening as it sounds, most bereaved parents are pleased to have these photographs to help them when remembering this short time together.

If you have decided on a name for your little one or used a name in pregnancy, that may now be your baby's name. It is natural to want to treat your baby with as much loving care as you would if they were alive and yet you may feel inhibited about doing so. Keeping the blanket or babygrow your baby wore and other mementoes such as hospital identity bands can also be a comfort in the years to come.

All of these suggestions may feel hard to imagine doing and they are not a must, but they may support you in the months and years ahead. It may not feel like you will ever feel anything but sad memories from this short time together and everything that happened, but, as the weeks and months go by, many parents tell me they feel proud of how they managed, and have an enduring love for the child they never had the chance to know.

As Elle Wright writes in *Ask Me His Name*, being able to hold her son Teddy and put him in a romper suit was what allowed her to feel like his mummy, even if only for a very short time: 'We washed him, changed him and dressed him in a romper suit and hat. I finally felt like a proper mummy, looking after him.'

Varied feelings and facing reality

There are very varied feelings for both parents when a baby dies at or around birth. There is often denial and a refusal to accept what has happened, especially in the very early stages. A mother on the SCBU at High Wycombe wanted some special time with her son after he had died. She picked up her little boy, cuddled him and then undid her nightie and brought him to her breast. As the unswallowed milk rolled down the little boy's unresponsive face, his mother's tears fell onto him. Those of us on the ward who saw this were concerned for her mental well-being and contacted the psychiatrist for the unit, asking if this should be happening. We were reassured that this mother needed time to fully appreciate that the baby she loved had died. It was only when he didn't swallow her milk that her tears began and she was able to realise that he really had.

Guilt and shame are also commonly felt by mothers whose baby has died, especially if she has had ambivalent feelings about the pregnancy or a relationship has ended during the pregnancy. It can be extremely hard for her to separate her feelings of guilt and shame from the facts of her grief. It is important to remember that almost every woman experiences moments of doubt and uncertainty about impending motherhood, and these thoughts do not in any way influence the way your pregnancy develops. And yet many pregnant mothers say they feel guilty for thinking something terrible that led to their baby's death. They wished they weren't pregnant or had regrets about the relationship they were in. While it is tempting to hold on to the idea that you may have somehow invited the pregnancy to end before time or caused complications with your inner doubts and worries, it will be more helpful in the long run if you can let go of this guilt which does not serve you. Thoughts are just that: thoughts. While you may well have thought something awful in the middle of the night when you were feeling overwhelmed, that does not mean in any way that you wanted or caused your baby's death. If you find yourself unable to let go of the idea that you were responsible, certain treatments like EMDR and cognitive behavioural therapy (CBT) can help you to move past recurring negative and unhelpful thoughts. Ask at your GP surgery or search your local council website to find recommended services.

Others may believe there is something fundamentally wrong with them that means their baby didn't want them. A mother whose baby son was stillborn told me how she felt he didn't want her to be his mummy. During her own childhood, her mother had been neglectful and had left her with her grandmother for long periods, usually when the mother had a new relationship, and often didn't return for months and even years. This woman, who as a child felt so deeply neglected, swore that, when her baby was born, she would never leave her baby and be every- thing to him that her mother had failed to be. She looked after herself very well in pregnancy and had a normal delivery, but her baby son was stillborn. The only way she could make sense of what happened in her despair was to think that he didn't want her to be his mummy. She told herself she wasn't good enough for the job.

Others may try to explain their baby's death as something they deserve. Another mum whose baby died just after he was born told me: 'It's my fault my baby died; it's because I hung the washing out.' Her husband had gone to work and told her to rest as the baby was due any day. But seeing the sun come out she had taken the opportunity to hang some sheets on the line to dry. This, she reasoned, was what had caused his death. Believing her decision to ignore her husband's advice had resulted in the complications that caused her baby's death gave her a way of understanding what had happened and someone to blame, even if that someone was herself. I couldn't persuade her otherwise – she felt certain she didn't keep him safe.

Bereaved parents have shown me that there is sometimes a comfort in taking responsibility for what has happened, as though feeling enough regret and remorse might make events less painful. This is a normal and very human response. It can take a long time to accept there was no grand design behind your baby's death and it was not something you had any control over at all, or deserved.

A Death at Home

Taking a newborn baby home is a far more frightening experience than many new parents anticipate. Even the most experienced nurse or doctor can feel very worried about something going wrong when they are suddenly left alone and in charge of their new baby. When the very worst of all our fears comes true and your baby dies at home, feelings of guilt and inadequacy are magnified, and it is common for parents to blame themselves for not having spotted a sign that their baby was unwell sooner. In fact, whether it is an accident or a sudden unexpected death, signs rarely show themselves and there is usually nothing more a parent could have done to keep their baby alive. But it can take many years, sometimes a lifetime, for parents to come to terms with this fact.

SIDS

When a baby dies at home without any explanation, it can often be some time before the mother or father discovers their little one is dead, especially if the baby dies in their cot during the night. Many of the families I have worked with have described how an older brother or sister alerted them to the baby sibling who would not wake up. Phone calls are made, ambulances are called and babies are taken to hospital, but if the baby has been dead for longer than a few minutes, there is very little medics can do. In addition to the cruelty of what has happened to their baby, parents must then leave their child's body at the hospital and are sent home, without the baby they loved so completely. This time can be extremely disorienting and parents often describe a feeling of everything being unreal. As with any death of a child, there is a huge amount of regret and blaming oneself: if only they had checked on them earlier or not slept so deeply themselves; if only they hadn't left the baby with a sitter. The 'if onlys' can seem infinite and it is only in learning to accept the facts of the events that you can begin to live with their death.

Jen, a mum who I supported after losing her first baby, Edward, to SIDS when he was only three months old, described the anguish and trauma of discovering her baby boy was unresponsive in the middle of the night:

'Mothers are meant to protect their children and I had this overwhelming guilt that I had failed my son. Even though doctors tried to reassure me that it wasn't my fault, the guilt and not knowing why a seemingly healthy baby could die unexpectedly like this only exacerbated my grief. It brought up lots of "why" questions which nobody could answer, so I turned inwards and blamed myself.

'In the early days of my grief, a future without Eddie seemed impossible. I felt I was existing but not living. Life was just about getting through the minutes, the hours and the days. I was in a limbo state, unable to be a mum and not mentally ready to go back to work. I had so much free time on my hands; I simply didn't know what to do. It was free time for the wrong reasons. I was meant to be a busy mum, living my life around my baby's life.'

SIDS deaths have decreased considerably over the years, but, sadly, in the UK almost 200 babies still die each year unexpectedly and, despite medical advances, in some cases doctors still do not know why. Unfortunately for parents whose baby has died in this way, there can often be further pain as they must also be interviewed by police and the minutiae of their last interactions with their baby scrutinised and relived. Sometimes evidence such as bottles and blankets are taken away and their baby's body becomes the subject of a coroner's case. Parents grieving the loss of their baby are now also under suspicion for the worst of crimes while their hearts are breaking beyond repair. It is one of the cruellest aspects of a baby's death in this way.

Sometimes a baby's body must undergo a post-mortem, and there is yet another level of agony to take on board. Knowing their baby's body must be cut open and investigated by a stranger is incredibly distressing. The only comfort is in knowing that it may help them to understand why their baby died and may help in medical understanding.

Jen set up the charity Teddy's Wish to help other parents whose baby's death is sudden and unexpected. See pages 168 and 175 for more details.

On post-mortems

If your child's death has happened unexpectedly and without an explanation, if your child died during an operation in a hospital or if their death is considered to be an unusual death such as a suicide or murder, your child's body will need to undergo a medical examination to establish the cause of death. A coroner usually instructs this as part of an inquest and it is so that everyone can know more about why and how your child died. Post-mortem examinations also help medical professionals understand more about certain conditions or diseases and can contribute towards better patient treatment in the future.

Despite the clear necessity and benefits of a post-mortem examination (sometimes also called an autopsy), the process can be extremely distressing for parents. While you are still coming to terms with the shock that your child has died, you now also need to allow your child's body to be surgically examined and inspected by a stranger. Unsurprisingly, many parents find this very hard.

There is very little anyone can say to improve on the facts of what happens in a post-mortem. A pathologist will make an incision down the front of your child's body and their organs are removed for inspection and examination. Another incision is usually made at the back of the head so that the pathologist can examine the brain. Sometimes it is not necessary to examine all of the organs and only a certain part of the body needs to be examined in this way. After the pathologist has completed their examination, the organs are returned to your child's body, the incisions are sewn up and your child will be returned to the funeral director or to you.

It can be frightening to think about this happening to your child and many parents feel worried about how their child's body will be treated during this procedure. It can be reassuring to remember that pathologists are highly qualified, meticulous and thoughtful doctors who always take their work extremely seriously and understand the great responsibility that comes with this unique job.

Two-year-old twins Betsy and William both died when they were crushed by a chest of drawers in their bedroom that they had climbed onto during what was meant to be nap time. Their father attended the coroner's inquest with trepidation; how the tragic accident had impacted their young bodies was not something he felt sure he wanted to hear about. But he listened intently to the pathologist's report and told me afterwards how the statement to the court had been extremely helpful and even moving for him to hear. He was so touched by the sensitive manner of the pathologist that, after the inquest, he went up to talk to the doctor to thank him and said: 'You were the last person that ever touched our precious children's bodies. I'm so glad you were so gentle and caring.' What had been a frightening prospect had in fact left him with some sort of comfort.

All post-mortems are different and will be carried out under different conditions for different reasons. Parents are allowed to be present during their child's post-mortem and, in some cases, you are allowed to ask for a representative to be there, such as your GP. There is good, clear information on the Citizen's Advice Bureau website and the website of the Royal College of Pathologists (see pages 172 and 174 for details). Your GP will also be able to support you with understanding the information and reports from your child's post-mortem.

However your baby has died, there are a few legal steps that need to be taken, such as registering their birth and obtaining a death certificate. For up-to-date advice in the UK, please go to www.gov.uk/when-someone-dies or contact one of the many charities listed on pages 172–176 for support.

Facing the World

We live in times when children of any age are not normally expected to die. But when a baby dies there can be an underlying sense that this loss is somehow less traumatic for their parents than the death of an older child. Society seems to place less value on the death of a baby. Perhaps this is because many more babies die than children, and a baby has not yet lived a life, formed connections with people or become a person with a distinct character. A baby hasn't come into any of their potential.

Grandparents and other well-meaning people may make comments about having another baby to help you 'get over' this one, or suggest it is not something you should dwell on for too long. This cultural downplaying of a baby's life can be extremely upsetting and infuriating for new parents, who have been ready to love their child for so long and would give anything to have the chance to get to know them.

Another common feeling in the early months of grieving for a baby is anger towards pregnant women you may know.

There is often anger in any kind of grief, but the uniquely visual reminder that a pregnant woman presents can be immensely painful. There is something in the lack of control over our own circumstances that leads to a sense of resentment in the presence of other expecting mothers. Envy for everything they have is common when your baby has died and you may find yourself wanting to avoid seeing other pregnant women for some time. This can present difficulties, especially among friends who are expecting babies around the same time, as is common, but is normal in grief and, gradually, with understanding, becomes less of a problem. Some grieving mothers are brave enough to find the right words to explain how they feel to their friend or sister/ sister-in-law and let them know that they hope it will pass.

There can also be resentment towards the parents of older children who have also died. Whether they are schoolchildren or older students, these children are often commemorated with plaques at their schools and written about in the local newspapers, their lives celebrated by their communities. The parents of babies or young children are rarely afforded these public acknowledgements of their grief or the specialness of their child. This sense of imbalance and unfairness is perfectly understandable. With the passing of time, many parents find that these feelings of resentment fade.

When friends don't say anything

Occasionally, people who have been very important to us can struggle to tell us how sorry they are for our loss. They feel for you, but they are frightened about upsetting you and will avoid seeing or contacting you. This can be especially true of people who are also expecting a new baby or having fertility treatment. As a bereaved parent, it can feel like you are being let down or even shunned by the people who are meant to care about you. There is not always a clear explanation for this, but it is often the case that the discomfort of your pain is more than they can bear. They may also have some unresolved grief of their own that limits their capacity for empathy. It is natural to resent this and to feel angry and upset with these people because it is you who is suffering such a great loss.

As unfair as it seems, you may need to be the person to do something about this if you want the friendship to last. A note or a text message to let friends know you would like to be in touch can be the olive branch you both need to move forward.

Often when a baby dies there are other children in the family who will need an honest and truthful explanation about the death of the sibling they have been looking forward to meeting and spending time with. Using simple language and answering their questions as honestly as you can is the best way forward here.

The parents of a little boy named Matthew (aged four) asked me for some help after his baby sister Katie died. He had been told that she had died and said that he would like to see her, but asked his parents what death would look like. When I met Matthew, I explained to him that his little sister would look very pale and have blue lips and that, if he wanted to touch her, she would be cold because her body didn't work anymore. When he saw her he didn't hesitate to hold her gently in his arms and immediately gave her a big kiss. Then he handed her back to me and got down off his chair ready to get on with his day with his parents who were taking him out.

Matthew's ease around his dead sister is an example of the enormous resilience and flexibility many children have in relation to death. Like adults, they move between behaviours of loss (kissing his sister) and restorative behaviour (walking off happily to enjoy his day), but often they do this more quickly and easily than adults. Their switching in and out should not be misinterpreted as anything other than just that; children are less able to stay in uncomfortable situations or sit with feelings in the way that adults can. We'll talk more about supporting children when a sibling dies in Chapter 7 (page 133).

When a Baby Dies: Some Things You Might Find Useful

The very worst has happened. There is nothing anyone can say or do that will ever be able to lessen the pain. However, bereaved parents have shown me that there are certain things you can do at this time that might be helpful to you. Some parents tend to find more comfort in loss-oriented activities, while others find restorative behaviour is more natural. For most parents, it is helpful to move between the two ways of being in grief – this is the natural ebb and flow of the dual process of grief that we explored on page 21.

Surround yourself with people who understand

Try to surround yourself with people who accept the devastation you are feeling and do not try to fix it. Avoid anyone who suggests you try not to be upset or tells you another baby will help you recover from this loss. You are grieving this baby and need those around you to be accepting and to listen and ask about your baby and your painful feelings without trying to make it better. It is up to you how you respond – you may not want to tell them anything and gradually that may change. If you find certain people difficult to be around, perhaps ask friends or a family member to create space between you.

Consider professional bereavement support

As well as good friends, it can help to find someone experienced in grief work who can help you explore your feelings at your pace. Sometimes caring family or friends are the most help, or the least. If you feel you need someone who understands grief, it's useful to ask at the hospital maternity department if they can recommend someone known to them or contact a bereavement charity, which may be able to offer financial support for some sessions. It is important to remember that there is nothing wrong with you – you are going through something emotionally very painful and there is no cure. There are many different types of counselling, and finding someone trained in understanding grief for a baby and who is interested in both you and your partner, if you have one, will be worth the investment of your time and money. There is advice and support on finding a grief counsellor on page 51.

Some relationships struggle as the weeks and months go by after a baby dies, and some couples find that a couples' counsellor helps them understand each other and the way they are both responding. We'll talk more about couples and parent relationships in Chapter 6 (page 117).

Keep mementoes

Today we know so much more about how important it is for parents in grief to create and hold on to memories of a baby who has died. Memories make the baby and the pregnancy real when parents feel they have nothing to show for all the love they still feel.

You can decide to keep a lock of your baby's hair and have your baby's footprints taken. This can be a very real comfort in the lonely years and months of grief without your baby. If your baby has died in hospital, you may be given a memory box to take home. Many parents choose to make or find their own boxes. It doesn't even need to be box; it can be a simple collection of items in a drawer, a small bag or a shelf at home with photographs and keepsakes on. You will find your own way of doing things. The important thing is that you don't underestimate the importance of these items and the memories they represent. As insignificant as they may seem, bereaved parents have taught me that they will be a comfort to you in the years to come.

Celebrate and remember birthdays and special dates

Whether it is their due date, their birthday or the day they died, or all of them, choose a date or dates that you can do something special on every year and remember your baby. It can be something as simple as going for a walk by yourself or inviting family members to come together to remember your baby. Whatever you choose to do, having a date devoted to remembering your baby can be a reassuring way to acknowledge their importance in your life.

Write your own birth story

If your baby died during or at birth, it can be helpful to write down your thoughts and memories of your pregnancy, their birth and how you feel about it all. You don't have to show anyone, unless you want to, but writing it down can be a helpful way of getting a clear picture in your mind of how everything happened and why. Labour can be a long and hectic process and, if we find ourselves in the throes of an emergency or extremely stressful situation, our emotions can take over and we can lose track of what is happening. This personal record of what happened and how you felt about it can be extremely helpful to return to when you feel confused or far away from the experience. Most hospitals offer parents an opportunity to meet with the medical and midwifery team who looked after you and your baby, usually a month or two after you go home, and this can be helpful in giving you clarity about how events unfolded.

Look after yourself

New mothers are very often physically and emotionally exhausted, and this applies whether your baby has died or not. The enormous physical changes mothers go through along with the ruthlessness of death and all its accompanying emotions can leave you feeling empty. Try to look after yourself if you can, eat well and drink plenty of water. Find time to do something for yourself, even if it is simply having a bath, getting your hair done or going for a walk to somewhere special to you. It won't take the pain away, but it might help you carry it.

However your baby has died, their life was precious and their death an enormous tragedy. The death of a baby is no less devastating for a parent than the death of a child who has lived a longer life. A lasting and powerful bond has been made between a mother and her child throughout pregnancy and, if they have lived outside the womb, the baby's short life. This bond and the love she has for her baby lasts forever, in the same way as any maternal or paternal attachment does, regardless of the child's age. A mother and father feel no less love for their child simply because they have died while still a baby. And the enormous sense of loss, for everything they will never know about their child, is felt as keenly as if they had known them a long time.

As Elle Wright writes in *Ask Me His Name*:

> 'Teddy will always be our firstborn child, the one who didn't get to come home. Nothing changes that. No matter what changes as we move forward, one more child or ten more children, there will always be one missing. Always one less. But he will always be loved and talked about, and we will carry his memory with us always too.'

Chapter 4

When a Younger Child Dies

'In between Henry's birth and his death was, of course, his life. That was my favourite part.'

Rob Delaney, *A Heart That Works*

When a baby is born, they remain physically connected to their mother until the umbilical cord is cut. The severing of this link between mother and child is the first step humans take in separating ourselves from our children. The work of parenting is in many ways a lifetime of continually and imperceptibly letting go of that now invisible cord – a gradual releasing of our child into the world, until such a time when they can be considered capable adults in their own right. Even then, we still hold the cord in our minds, and every tiny piece that slips out of our hands is a moment and a memory etched – an invisible connection that remains between us and them for all of our lifetimes.

When a child who lives at home and who we no longer consider to be a baby, but who is still fully engaged in the activities and needs of childhood, dies, parents find they are still holding on to a great length of that invisible cord. In this sense, the death of a child can feel particularly confusing. Their work as parents has only just begun; they are still holding a long reel of cord in their arms. What are they to do with it now? It is a grief for all the memories and experiences they have already shared with their child, but also for the future they have not yet lived through with them; a grief that looks backwards and forwards with equal amounts of pain and sorrow.

Parenting a younger child is still enormously physical and our days are full and focused around our children. If they are very young, we are constantly watching them, chasing toddlers around the house, making sandwiches or putting bubbles in their baths. Children can be especially excited by their new-found mobility at around two years old and begin to realise they are separate beings from their mother. They can become exceptionally inquisitive and adventurous, and often surprise us by doing something unexpected that they haven't done before. The so-called terrible twos is a period when we typically see a lot of accidents involving young children.

Two-year-old Conwy was playing in the garden on the day he died. The back door was open and little Conwy was happily toddling in and out, bringing in stones to show his parents. Everyone knew the garden was completely safe and Conwy could not come to any harm while he was enjoying making his discoveries. However, after a short while, his parents realised Conwy had not come back in as expected and they all got up to look for him outside. His father, Simon, ran down a sloping lawn to an area of the garden no one ever went to, where there was a small pond surrounded for safety by strong wire fencing. There he saw with horror that, in his curiosity, Conwy had tried to climb the wire fencing and toppled over into the shallow pond. His father pulled him up out of the reeds, but it was too late to save him as he had quietly drowned. In a matter of seconds, the family had gone from having a busy little boy in their life to knowing that life would never be the same again. (Simon and I went on to make a short film together about accidental deaths and young children. *The Danger Age* can be viewed on the ALMT website, see page 171, or by searching for the title on YouTube.)

Teenagers can also become great risk-takers and this is another age when we tend to encounter the sad consequences of curiosity and misadventure more than at other times. Drug overdoses, accidents, falls and pranks gone wrong can all lead to devastating consequences. Arthur Cave was 15 when he tragically died. Arthur had experimented with LSD for the first time and, after becoming disoriented with the effects of the hallucinogenic drug, had fallen off a cliff near his home in Brighton. (His father, songwriter Nick Cave, went on to create The Red Hand Files, which has become a wonderful, supportive resource for bereaved families everywhere and the details are on page 164.)

Sadly, some young children die suddenly and unexpectedly, and parents may never have any idea why their child has died. In December 2013, when her Christmas presents were all wrapped and under the tree, Nikki's two-year-old daughter Rosie died without warning:

'She had been happy and healthy, scooting around the zoo the day before and in the morning we found her in her bed. She'd died during the night and we had no idea why. We still don't know why all these years later, despite a full investigation and even genetic testing – the best science can offer.

'It felt shocking and impossible that when we left hospital that day and for the weeks and months after, doctors couldn't tell us why Rosie died.'

As we touched on in Chapter 2, after Rosie died, Nikki co-founded the charity SUDC UK to support families affected by SUDC, raise awareness and fund research to help prevent further deaths. There's more about SUDC UK in Chapter 8 (see page 166).

Whatever age our children are, if they are not yet adults, parents are usually busy organising their lives, dropping them off and picking them up, arranging time with their friends and doing all the things that parents do. We love them for who they are and the unique personality that is emerging, but we also love them visibly and protectively, always trying to stay one step ahead of them. Whether it is an eye on the edge of the kerb coming up or a gentle warning about the dangers of the online world, our love for a child who lives with us is active and physical, all-consuming and particularly tiring in its duties and requirements.

Equally, that child's love for us, their parent, is as yet not entirely tamed by social conventions and the business of being an adult. If they are little, they run to us when they see us, hold our hands to cross the road and sit on our laps when they are tired. They sob when they are sad and lash out at us when they are angry. Older children and teenagers also do plenty of their own acting out. Their mess and their moods are as present in our lives as when they were small – a reflection of the changes taking place in their inner world. Whether they are at preschool or college, or anywhere in between, much of their work – the work of growing up to being young adults – is learning to tame and manage these feelings. We think of adults who cannot control their emotions as childish. And yet to be around the unashamed and unedited feelings of our children is one of life's greatest privileges. Adults rarely share between them such uninhibited and freely given feelings as those we receive from the children we share a home and a life with. Learning to live without, and losing proximity to, the kind of love we receive from and take part in with a child is one of the hardest and greatest aspects of the grief parents are tasked with when their child dies. It is one of the many ways they must now learn to live as a bereaved parent.

A Conspicuous Absence

A child who lives at home is always a big presence in their parents' and siblings' lives, from the noise and mess they make to the time they require, whether providing lifts or helping with homework. When they die, it is not only the person parents miss, but the many sensory and physical aspects of living with them that are no longer part of their lives.

Many parents find they become aware of the sounds they no longer hear when a child who lives at home dies: the sounds of a little one who is constantly chattering; the banging of the front door that signals their child is home; the noise of an enthusiastic gamer playing online with friends; the cries of a dejected toddler who wants to play with their siblings; or the music blasting from a teenager's bedroom. The sounds that tell you your child is safe at home become painfully conspicuous by their absence when that child dies. Becoming accustomed to quieter days and nights is extremely hard for parents. Many find themselves believing they can hear familiar sounds, before realising they could not have, and this can go on for many years.

'We miss the noise of being a family of four,' says a mum whose eight-year-old son Henry died suddenly from undiagnosed encephalitis, shortly before the coronavirus pandemic, in November 2019. 'Our grief is a lonely, empty place, with all that was once familiar gone.' Henry's 11-year-old sister Giselle also missed the fun and busy-ness of her little brother and found his absence very difficult, as it was during the pandemic and she was at home with her parents. Her mum said:

> 'The hardest thing for Giselle was not having Henry around while we were out of action with Covid. Henry loved being at home and they would disappear for hours in a world of their imagination, whether Playmobil in the attic, Lego cities in bedrooms or building dens or assault courses in the garden.'

Other small and often unexpected things take parents by surprise when they are no longer part of everyday life after the death of a child: favourite food on the shopping list that no longer needs to be bought; seeing a jacket in the shops that you think might suit them even though they are no longer here; the lack of mess; the laundry basket that is no longer full; dates and times of the year, such as the start of a new school term or the Halloween celebrations they once enjoyed so much … These are all grief's tiny yet often vicious pokes that keep your pain at the surface. They can hit you in the solar plexus or give you a crippling headache at any moment, and take your breath away with grief as fresh as the day it happened. And yet they are moments that are often undetectable to anyone but you.

Many people don't understand that, as a bereaved parent, you take these blows every day, wherever you are, whatever you are doing, for years and years to come. There is a huge amount of physical strength involved in living with these moments – the sheer energy it takes for your body to go through and recover from something as seemingly insignificant as being confronted by a noise or a smell. When your child dies before becoming an adult you may find yourself exhausted by what feels like an unrelenting challenge, just to get through each day, month and year in one piece. Like many aspects of this pain, the intensity does fade over the years, as you become more familiar and able to cope with your grief.

Some parents, especially in the very early stages of grief, find themselves continuing to behave as though their child is alive. The mind plays tricks in grief; what has happened is sometimes too big to take in immediately. Routines and rituals that were an important part of your day, and your child's day, may feel important to continue. In the first hours and days, you might choose to visit your child's body in the chapel of rest to bring them pyjamas or simply to sit and read to them, for example. You might repeat this slow, letting-go routine more than once. This is a normal and very human response to such an enormous loss and is helpful for grieving parents struggling to come to terms with what has happened. Although it is hard for those around you to witness, this behaviour rarely needs to be halted; it is something most will eventually come to stop of their own accord. As time goes on, you might continue to set a place at the table for your child, hang stockings at Christmas and make cakes on their birthday. These are all ways of remaining close to your child and are in no way unhealthy or worrisome. You are continuing to parent your child, and it will eventually help you to come to terms with the fact of their death.

Feelings of Guilt and Self-Blame

Parents often want to blame themselves for the death of a child who has not reached adulthood. A huge amount of the pain parents carry with them when their child has died is tangled up with guilt and a sense of shame for what they believe they could or should have done to prevent their death. You might feel you should have put them in a coat that made them more visible, spent more time with them talking about how to behave around drugs or pushed harder for more help from their doctors or medical teams.

However they have died, it can take many years to accept the choices and decisions you may or may not have made before they died, and to accept that you did what you could, with the resources you had, at the time; that you were good enough.

Daniel's mum had talked to her son, who was 14 when he died, about the dangers of taking drugs: 'I'd had a conversation specifically with Dan about ecstasy. It's one of the things you do as a parent, isn't it? I was more worried about him being safe on his bike than at a party with friends,' says his mum. 'I love you Mum; I promise I won't die,' joked Daniel as he left for what his mum thought was a party at his friend's house. Daniel died later that night after taking ecstasy at an illegal rave. (His story has been turned into a play that now features on the GCSE drama syllabus – see page 163.)

There are usually also a lot of feelings of guilt, not only for the things parents believe they could have done or not done, but for the way they were feeling and behaving, either inwardly or outwardly, in the minutes and hours, even days, before their child died – for example, a parent who complained about the ordinariness of their day at home with a small child and left them with a sitter so that they could go out, or who felt disappointed in their child's abilities and pushed them too hard to succeed. If their child had additional needs or a disability, many parents feel guilty for lacking patience before their child died. Perhaps they just didn't love being a parent enough, and their child's death is their punishment.

The just-world hypothesis – the idea that we always get what we deserve – becomes especially powerful when a young child dies and many parents feel they were never truly good enough to deserve the beautiful child they had been raising. As difficult as it is, your work now is in coming to accept that there is nothing different you could or should have done; you did what you did, and there is no meaning or divine punishment intended behind your child's death. It is a senseless tragedy and it has happened to you. It is the very worst luck of the draw; one that will last a lifetime. Only by staring these uncompromising facts in the face can you begin to get back to the business of loving and parenting your child, at least in your heart and mind, for the rest of your life.

Other People and Facing the World

When a child dies before reaching adulthood, there are very often other adults in the family who also feel devastated by their death – whether that's grandparents who might have been providing childcare so you could work or a special aunt whose own children were your child's much-loved cousins. They are devastated for you, but also for themselves and the loss of the joy and meaning your child brought to their own lives.

Sometimes these relationships are already rather delicate. Families are complex and only grow more so over time. When a child who is loved within a family network dies, the already strained relationships you have worked so hard to maintain can be tested to their limits. You may feel that others are too vocal or visible with their grief, to the extent that you begin to resent the grandparents and others who want to share your sorrow. It can feel as though you are being robbed of the right to the enormous grief you are feeling. When grief is all there is left, you can feel a need to own the experience and may not wish to let others share your desperation.

Other people's grief can also feel like an unnecessary burden at this time – the need to comfort a weeping grandparent or a devastated aunt can be more than you can bear. Tempers are frayed to their very edges. This is all a normal part of grieving for a child. Families can and do fall out in the aftermath; it happens more often than not. Feelings are so strong and running so high that certain dynamics and personalities may simply not survive the turbulence of grief. Often, with time, things can return to a more familiar setting, but equally, for some families, there is no way back to the way things once were.

Other children who live at home can also be especially demanding for parents in grief. So much energy is taken up by grieving, by thinking about and missing your child. Every morning the day begins by waking up and remembering what has happened, starting the process of being a bereaved parent over again, every day, for all of your life. It can be very difficult to then find the patience and time for other children, to be forgiving and understanding when they make mistakes or behave in a challenging way.

At the same time, other children may actually become more demanding, physically and emotionally, as they also come to terms with not only the absence of their sibling, but the parents and family they once knew that is now forever altered. It is very common for children and teenagers in this situation to 'play up' perhaps because they are missing their sibling or because they want to attract attention from a parent who is distant and lost in their grief. (There is more advice on supporting children and siblings in Chapter 7 on page 133.)

Friends and other families can also become a problem if they fear talking to you about your child and your grief. Much of a younger child's life is about their friendships and activities, and, as parents, we often find friendship in the families who our child spends time with. Finding yourself on the outside of the once-familiar WhatsApp groups for lift shares and birthday presents can add an extra sense of isolation and torment. Others might avoid talking to you, remove you from the chat or take your name off a list for sports day. They do this because they fear provoking your sadness. It holds a mirror to their own greatest fears. While it is never your job to educate others in how to respond to your grief, it can help if you are able to let people know that you do want them to acknowledge your child's death and to talk to you about your child. So often other people want to avoid making you upset, and yet it is only by allowing yourself to be upset that you can begin to live again.

When a Younger Child Dies: Some Things You Might Find Useful

The death of a young child brings a uniquely painful grief. Children give and receive love in the purest and most uncomplicated way, and, as parents, we must now accept that we will never get to watch that love grow. Nothing can change the heartbreaking death of a child who has not yet become an adult, but you may find some of the following suggestions can help you, either now or in the future.

Say a final goodbye to your child

If it is at all possible to see your child's body, to hold them and touch them after their death, and you feel able to, it can be comforting for you in the future to do this. The sense of denial and shock that you are experiencing will not be diminished by this significant act, but in the future it can help you to fully believe that your child has died. Seeing your dead child's body is never easy and, if it can be arranged, be sure to surround yourself with kindness and support. An experienced healthcare professional can prepare you for what you will see and make sure you are ready.

Try making something

Some parents keep their child's precious possessions and favourite toys, and making a memory box is an especially popular way to create something you can return to when you feel you need to spend time with your child and your grief. There are no rules about what you can put inside a memory box or what it looks like. Or you might choose to create something unique from a favourite item of your child's clothing or bedding.

One mum used her son Benny's favourite shirt to make a picture. Benny loved his little green and blue shirt so much that, when he died, she could not bring herself to part with it.

93

Although not an experienced seamstress, she mended a little tear in his shirt and cut out a square of the fabric around the tear. She sewed a felt heart on top and embroidered it with Benny's name. She then framed the square of fabric and hung it on the wall at home so she can see it and walk past it every day.

You don't have to sew or make a picture, and if you do it doesn't need to be perfect. But the process of actively and purposefully making something to honour your child can be restorative and give you something to focus on when it feels like nothing matters anymore.

Make plans for the difficult times

The end of the day and the early evening can often be a very difficult time for bereaved parents, who really miss the routines of teatime and bath time that come with young children. Being aware and mindful of this time and how it might be especially difficult for you will help you to manage. Crafting, reading, walking the dog, journaling and doing exercise are all great ways to look after yourself during this difficult time. It can be extremely tempting to turn to alcohol, but while it might provide a temporary distraction, it rarely helps in the long run. Try to treat yourself with the same love and dignity that you would wish for someone else in your shoes.

Collage your grief

Something many parents find hard, especially in the early months and years of life after their child has died, is understanding and making sense of their own behaviour and that of their partner's, if they have one. Understanding that we all engage in two types of behaviour – the dual process model we explored on page 21 – can explain why some days you only want to cry and stay at home, while on others you might want to go for a run or start a new project. Especially helpful in learning to understand your grief and make sense of your behaviours is the old-fashioned art of collaging. Collect a pile of old magazines and newspapers and sit with some scissors, glue and a piece of card, and choose images that help you create a collage image of all the different ways you feel and behave. You can use words and pictures; it doesn't need to look perfect. The end result will give you a visual snapshot of the way you are managing your grief and some of the images you choose to include might surprise you. If you are struggling to connect with a partner or a family member, collaging can also be a useful communication tool – a way of describing your grief when words are hard to find.

Stay connected

Remaining connected to your child's friends and the activities they enjoyed can feel hard at first, but it can also be joyful and comforting to stay close to the link and bond that your child shared with them. If and when you are ready, you might choose to find a way to participate in those activities or groups that your child was part of. It could be creating a sports trophy in their name or raising funds for new equipment at their school. You will know what works for you and what will bring you comfort in the years to come.

Lean on your friends

Friends are incredibly important, and you will know who the people are that you can lean on. The people who you can walk with in silence, who aren't afraid to talk about your child and say their name, and who will cook you nourishing food without expecting to stay and eat with you, are the people you need around you.

When in doubt, go for a walk

Grieving parents have taught me that walking in nature, alone or with a friend, for an hour or for ten minutes, is one of the best ways to bring yourself into the present and get some relief from the painful ruminations of grief. You leave the house feeling one way and come home feeling another and, in this way, a walk

95

provides the fastest and most effective way to do something for yourself in grief.

Grief after the death of a young child is devastating – it is a grief for all that has happened in their short time with you, and all that can never happen; a pain that pulls at you from all directions. It will take many years to find a way to manage this loss and to accept that your child will never become an adult, but, eventually, over time, many parents have told me they are able to take their child through life with them, just as they are.

> 'Angus came into my life and opened my soul to indescribable love. We shared a world together that can never be recreated. I miss his gentleness and the magic he showed me how to find in everyday life. I am so sad that he did not get the chance to live the wonderful life that would have been rightfully his. I wish I had had the chance to meet the person he would become. My hope is that one day I may be so lucky. Til then I carry his love in my heart. At least I never have to say goodbye.'
>
> **Kara Lawson,** *Farewell My Child*

Chapter 5

When an Older or Adult Child Dies

'I long for her to walk through the door now. There are so many things I'd love to talk to her about. She roared with laughter all the time. She was my father's granddaughter. My son could make her laugh to the point of hysteria, almost. She was the most joyous person to be around.'

Sir Richard Attenborough, *Guardian,*
6 September 2008

If a younger child belongs to us, then an older child belongs to the world. Whether they are still in education or have a career and even a family of their own, play in a band or a team, or are simply part of a friendship group, most older and adult children are members of their own personal communities outside of their original family unit. These independences are usually a source of great pleasure and pride to most parents, as they reassure us that our children can enjoy relationships, make connections and develop skills without us being around. They show us that our child can live successfully and safely when they are out in the world – and that, when we are no longer here to protect them, they will be able to survive. Being a parent to an adult child is about letting go of the invisible umbilical cord as far as it is possible to let it go, yet still being happy in the knowledge that your child is on the other end of it somewhere in the world, even if you can't see them.

Parenting an older child can also be about great friendship. Whether you are the kind of parent who likes to describe themselves as their child's friend or not (not all parents do), being in your child's life as they become an adult will involve some level of friendship and mutual respect. The decision to spend time with each other, to spend Christmas or other special occasions together or share family holidays with adult children often comes down to a basic mutual appreciation and an enjoyment of each other's company. Whether you share similar tastes, make each other laugh or enjoy doing the same things together, the bond a parent shares with an older child is often to do with a friendship that has formed over the years of the now-adult child's lifetime, and is therefore one of the longest friendships both parent and child can ever have. The death of an adult child means not only grieving your child, but someone you had grown to know and cherish as a person in their own right. They had also lived with you and spent years around the most authentic version of yourself; they knew you, possibly better than anyone else. With their death comes the loss of being known and clearly seen by someone very precious.

For some parents, the parent–adult–child relationship can mean great disagreements and disappointments – it can be as much about distance and relationships turned sour as it can be about friendship and mutual respect. A happy relationship in childhood may have been spoiled by trauma in the teenage years; many parents talk of regret and remorse about how life at home had been during these typically very challenging years for all families. Money, parents widowed and new step-parents invited into the fold, houses sold and new siblings born can all influence how older children and their parents relate as the years go by. The death of an adult child in a situation of estrangement or strained relationships is no less harrowing for the parent, who still loves their child as much as they did on the day they were born. You are always their parent, regardless of your relationship with your child.

By the time your child is an adult, you have had to let them go many times over, but bereaved parents have taught me that this does not make their death any less painful or somehow easier to live with. All the years of loving them and everything they have meant to you can feel like the world's greatest waste.

A Shift in Identity

To have watched your child grow into adulthood is to have witnessed and been a proud part of many important milestones in their life – education and extra-curricular achievements, leaving home, first jobs, first home, first child – and also to have been there for their great disappointments, jobs lost and relationships ended, hopes of all kinds dashed. To be a parent to an adult child is to see an almost infinite amount of possible milestones on the horizon, good and bad, high and low, and to feel closely identified with all of them, through your child.

When an adult child dies, so do your own associations with their milestones and their journey through life. With their death, your identity can be forever changed and you no longer have the years ahead of you that you once anticipated, while the journey behind you is forever tainted with sadness. Occasions that you might have once relished and looked forward to, such as religious holidays and birthdays, might no longer have the same meaning. Roles you played as a parent, confidante or sounding board, even being the famous 'bank of mum and dad', are gone and, with them, perhaps parts of your own identity.

Hannah, 26, had purchased her first flat and moved in earlier in the year. On 22 December, her parents, Howard and Dee, drove the few miles from their family home to pick her up; she was going back to spend Christmas with them, her siblings and other close family. They were mildly concerned that they had not heard from Hannah that morning, but nothing could have prepared them for the devastating shock of finding her lying peacefully in bed, where she had died during the night.

The following few weeks passed by in an agonising blur for her family. Hannah's body was taken to a mortuary, where because of the Christmas and New Year period, her family weren't permitted to see her. The seasonal delay meant they also spent several weeks waiting for the post-mortem and pathologist's report; eventually, they were told that Hannah's death had been a result of sudden adult death syndrome (SADS). Her parents had never heard of this, but it is the equivalent of SIDS and SUDC in that there is no warning and no apparent reason for, or cause of, this death when it happens. The one tiny source of comfort to Hannah's family was that she had not suffered.

Howard said:

> 'The first thing I saw when I went into her flat that day was the big bag of presents that she had bought for the family; she loved the present opening ceremony on Christmas Day morning and, although they were all now adults, always insisted that she and her siblings still received packed, personalised stockings. Now Christmas has a profoundly poignant feel to it for all of us.'

The death of an adult child can also create a significant gap in a mature family system and leave elderly parents feeling unsupported and unsure of their own future. Depending on how old they are, an adult child has sometimes become a pillar of the family, perhaps hosting family events or providing the expertise for something within the family, such as offering financial support and care to their parents. As well as the enormous grief they must wake up to every morning, some parents also now feel afraid and unsure of their own futures. Who will be there for them and look after them?

Other children, who may or may not yet be adults, will also go through enormous shifts in their self-identity and the place they occupy in the family. In all families where there is more than one child, the death of a child creates huge ripples and often very complex feelings among the siblings and others who are left behind. There is more about siblings and their experience in Chapter 7 (page 133).

Taking care of what remains when an adult child dies can also sometimes create shifts in the identity you had given them. If adult children can be our friends, they can also sometimes reveal themselves to be strangers in their death. If they did not have a partner or a family of their own, you may find yourself sorting through their belongings or selling their property and, in the process, making discoveries about them that you were never expecting to. Sexual orientation and preferences, drug use, financial problems, complicated relationships and other issues they may have tried to shield you from can all come to light with their death. The shock of their death is layered with truths about them that you may never have known or wanted to know. Talking these things through with an experienced bereavement counsellor will help you manage your feelings in this situation, although, like everything in grief, it is likely to take time. (There is advice on finding a bereavement counsellor on page 51.)

Complicated Feelings

Even though your older child had a life of their own and may have left home, when they die, some parents feel responsible for their death. In their distress, parents may blame themselves – wondering what they could have done differently that may have prevented their child from making the decisions or being in the circumstances that led to their death. For some, the guilt is crippling; even though it is seldom justified, guilt can be the self-inflicted punishment that grieving parents feel they deserve as part of their grief. For those experiencing it, the adage that guilt is a wasted emotion is not always true. In my work with bereaved parents, I've learned that it is something parents may want to actively experience; they may need to feel punished and for some time. Taking the blame in this way may give them the connection to their child and helps them cope with the enormous burden of their overwhelming grief.

The death of an older child can be especially confusing and complicated for their parents. So much of being able to grieve lies in accepting the reality of what has happened; it's why it is often helpful for parents to see their child's body and spend time with their son or daughter before saying goodbye, if they can. Remembering this experience, as painful as it is, can also enable parents to know and feel that they did everything they could right from their child's birth to after their death. This is why it is important when possible to establish and visually confirm the circumstances of your child's death. Knowing and seeing the truth helps you believe that what you are told is true and to feel that nothing has been hidden from you, to know that there was nothing more you could have done.

I learned the importance of identifying older children who have died from the complications that followed the *Marchioness* disaster of 1989. I was involved in helping the families of the 51 young adults who drowned when the party boat they were on sank in the River Thames. Many of their families were never allowed to see their bodies; the coroners' office, police and pathologists decided that visual identification of bodies recovered from the Thames would be too distressing for them. Decades later, many families are still deeply traumatised by the lack of control they had over their children's bodies.

Although what happened after the *Marchioness* is all unfortunately true, it is also exactly the kind of terrible nightmare parents who have not had the chance to see their child's dead body can create in their minds. Families whose children have died abroad may also struggle with such problems as language barriers and cultural differences, and those I have supported after a death abroad have taught me that they can't settle until they know what has happened. Having the support of the Foreign Office and trained liaison officers is vital in these circumstances.

Also especially difficult, and often not recognised, is the guilt felt by parents who care for an adult child with additional needs or a life-limiting illness. Many people assume it is a relief for them when their child dies, but most parents only feel bereft. Their child has been everything to them, required their constant care and so much of their time and energy that it is very difficult to adjust to life without them. Many parents feel a sense of regret and shame for all the normal stresses and strains they may have felt and shown in their daily lives with their child.

No one believes a parent is responsible for these tragic deaths or for having natural feelings of frustration around disability and life-limiting illnesses, but I've seen that, for those of you left behind, there is now a deep void that many people will never understand. The need to stay emotionally close to your child, and the meaningful connection you shared with them, even if it means shouldering the blame, is strong. It is only with time and the arrival of newer, happier experiences and moments that these feelings become more familiar and their crippling power over you begins to recede.

Grieving an Adult Child as a Grandparent

If your adult child has died and you are a grandparent to their child or children, the grief you experience can be especially complex. You not only grieve for your child, who, despite being an adult, remains forever your child even in their death, but also you are likely to feel enormous sorrow and responsibility for your grandchild or grandchildren, and the parent they will never know. An unwanted and unwelcome shift in your entire life's purpose must now take place, from proud grandparent to grieving parent, at a time when you may have been expecting that the hard work of life might begin to ease.

Extra complications can feature in your grief as a grandparent. Geography can present grieving grandparents with problems. If you live far away from your grandchild, you may feel an urge to move to be closer to them and, in doing so, be closer to the child you are grieving. But you may not be able to do this easily if, for example, you have not retired yet or have other children close by. Trying to support and have a relationship with your grandchild, who will also be in grief, at a long distance is extremely hard and yet so important.

You might also find that contact with your child's partner or ex-partner can become strained. For many families, this is not an issue and everyone finds they can pull together in grief. Many parents talk of the deep love they feel for their dead child's partner and close friends, and often the feelings are reciprocated; a link to a past life that everyone wants to hold on to. However, if relationships with your adult child or their partner have been strained in life, the death of an adult child can set in motion a battle. Sometimes it is spoken and sometimes unspoken, as bereaved partners (and often their parents, the other grandparents) try to establish new family dynamics with the grieving parents of the partner who has died. There is anger and resentment in most grief anyway, and to deal with these new challenges as everyone feels the searing unfairness of the situation can be deeply painful. There can be the temptation to alienate grieving grandparents and block access, especially if relationships are already difficult. You, the grandparent, may have had ambivalent feelings about your child's partner to begin with, and now face a lifetime of being involved with them without your child's presence to temper your feelings.

Many parents grieving adult children also talk of their grief being eclipsed by that of the dead child's partner or even ex-partner. Your grandchild's remaining parent will also usually be the person police and funeral directors liaise with, leaving many grandparents feeling left out and isolated from the decisions and processes that take place after their child's death. Many of the grieving grandparents I have worked with find this very difficult because their child is forever their child and they wish very much to be able to take care of them in their last moments of life and in death.

Enormous amounts of empathy and patience are required to maintain harmonious links between the family where the grand-child or grandchildren live, and the family unit where the parent who died was once also a child. It can sometimes be useful to ask other relatives or another older child to be a mediator in these circumstances. Every family is different and only you will know the best way to manage these difficulties.

When an Older Child Dies By Suicide

Suicide is the main cause of death in people under 35 in the UK, and around three-quarters of those who choose to end their own lives are boys and young men. Suicide brings with it a terrible sense of rejection for parents; the sense that their child did not want to be with them. Parents also feel shame, about how other parents might judge them, and guilt that they had not spotted the signs that something was wrong. Sadly, suicides and the inquests that follow them are also more likely to be reported in the local and national newspapers, giving grieving parents an extra layer of pain and suffering to cope with.

So much remains misunderstood about suicide and why a child of any age might end their own life. It is widely assumed that, for most who take this irreversible step, suicide is the final point in a struggle with poor mental health. However, it is also the case that some suicides can come as a complete shock to the families of those who end their lives, and there can be no history of mental illness or suggestion as to why it might have happened.

Whether there is a clear explanation or very little evidence to explain anything about it, suicide is a death that comes with a litany of agonising mysteries for the parents who are left to grieve their child: why did their child choose to end their life? What more could they have done to prevent them from succeeding? How could their child have been so unhappy and how could they not have known? Were they in physical pain at the end? Did they really mean to do it? There are so many unanswered questions for parents. It is an incredibly difficult death to learn to live with and often it is only because of other children or a partner that parents feel they even want to carry on.

As for any parent who learns that their child has died, there is an initial, visceral reaction to their death. For some parents, this is news delivered to them by an official at the door; for others, this can mean discovering their child's body in extremely disturbing and visually difficult-to-process circumstances. If you have not been the person to find your child, you will have been required to identify their body and this can be equally distressing, an experience many parents describe as feeling unreal. These experiences can create a trauma reaction that can stay with you for many years and be triggered by seemingly innocuous things; the sight of a certain type of car, a certain time of day or the mention in passing of a particular substance. It is impossible to know how or what these triggers might be and how they might affect you if your child has died by suicide. Nothing can ever remove them entirely from your mind, but specialist therapies such as EMDR can help to reduce the distressing impact of these triggers over time for some parents (see page 43).

While most deaths by suicide share very little common ground, one thing that is almost certain you will feel if your child has ended their life is the need to blame yourself for not having spotted the signs sooner or done more to prevent it. The guilt, even if it is not remotely justified, can stay with parents forever. When Mary's youngest son, Paul, 16, ended his own life she wrote in a letter to him:

> 'I have racked my brains and seen all sorts of signs we missed. I wish you had told me how desperate you had become. We could have helped you. You took all the pain and worry on to yourself and this is so typical of you, wanting to be no bother to those around you. I will never forgive myself for not knowing how bad things were.'

For many parents, there is also a sense of shame, a worry about what you believe others must think of you. As Jasper's mum, Rebecca, describes, she felt sure others regarded her as a bad mother after her 18-year-old son killed himself: 'I had times when I felt extraordinary shame. I felt sure people were thinking it was my fault; that it must have been something I did. I must have been a bad mother, otherwise he wouldn't have wanted to die.'

The way people spoke about her son also seemed to change and she noticed how people wanted to blame him for being selfish while others simply stopped mentioning him at all:

> 'There seemed to be a need to blame him. People would tell me and my husband Louis how cross they were with Jasper for what he'd done to his siblings and us, his parents. It was as if blaming him was a warped way of protecting us. Other family members stopped even saying his name in case it

caused upset. But I was never cross with him. I just needed to understand. I kept repeating events over and over in my mind. Louis likened it to travelling down a river and finding ourselves stuck in these whirlpools of "if only"s, going over things and around and around until we had to let go of what we couldn't answer. Only then could we move a little further downstream.'

It can feel extremely isolating when your child ends their own life and you may find that, while some friends are extremely supportive, a few of the families and friends you once took for granted may distance themselves, perhaps because they find it too difficult to know what to say or how to behave, or perhaps because they are frightened. Suicide can be a frightening experience for everyone it touches. Some family and friends may show their support through their actions, for example by holding a fundraising walk or bike ride. Sometimes parents who are bereaved by this kind of death find that it is other parents whose child has also ended their life who they can talk and relate to more easily, and this is why support groups are so important for parents experiencing this kind of grief.

If you have other children, it is likely they will also be feeling a complex range of emotions and, depending on their age and experience, may not necessarily be able to fully understand the way they feel in the wake of their sibling's suicide. Feelings of abandonment are common, as is the sense that they have been left alone in the family and been given extra duties of childhood that they did not ask for or want. There is anger and frustration, disbelief and confusion, and, like you, they are likely to want to blame themselves for not preventing their sibling's death. They may feel frightened about their own future and worry that they might also be overcome by suicidal thoughts and feelings, and this can create significant anxiety for them and for you. It is important that everyone in the family receives counselling and children will also benefit from meeting other young people in their position via support groups and networks such as the Student Grief Network (see page 163 for details).

There are a few charities offering specialist support to parents and siblings who are bereaved by suicide, in particular Survivors of Bereavement by Suicide (SOBS), Winston's Wish and Compassionate Friends. Details are included in Useful Information (pages 172–176). Some local authorities also run excellent support groups for parents who are bereaved by suicide.

On inquests

When someone of any age dies by suicide, there is a legal requirement for a coroner to hold a public hearing known as an inquest, and this is held at a Coroner's Court. The coroner will open the inquest very shortly after your child's death and then the hearing will happen at a later date, once all the evidence and information relating to your child's death has been gathered. Depending on the circumstances and whether there has been a police investigation, this can be months and sometimes longer after the inquest is initially opened. At the hearing, you will hear evidence from people such as the doctor and pathologist and anyone else who may have had contact with your child around the time of their death. If there has been a police investigation, all the details and statements of anyone else involved will be heard at the inquest. You may also be asked to make a statement. This is because the coroner needs to be satisfied that your child intended to end their life.

Because they are public meetings, anyone can attend an inquest and sometimes this means that members of the press and other people you may not wish to be there are present; this is understandably very difficult for parents who are already dealing with enormous grief. It also means your child's death can be freely reported in the media without your consent or involvement. Inquests are also very formal and business-like procedures, which are often at odds with the kind and sympathetic interactions you may have had with your police family liaison officers and other services that may have supported you after your child's death. In short, while inquests can be very helpful for establishing clarity, they can also often be re-traumatising for parents whose child has died by suicide.

There is very little anyone can do or say to make this difficult procedure any easier for parents. Having someone you trust attend the inquest with you, such as a close friend or counsellor, can be helpful and can ensure that, at the end of inquest, the press are supplied with accurate details of your child's name and age provided by the family. It is an unfortunate but necessary part of the legal process around suicide in the UK.

Jasper's mum was comforted by the thought that her son's inquest was the last time he would ever need to be in the hands of the system and the words of her husband who, at the end of the proceedings, turned to her and said: 'We can take him home now.'

When an Adult Child Dies: Some Things You Might Find Useful

When our adult child dies, we lose not only a child, but someone who has been with us for a lifetime. Our memories, shared experiences and love stretch deep and wide, and learning to live in the world without the child we have known so well is enormously difficult. Bereaved parents have shown me that, with time and the care and support of those around you, it is possible to carry those memories with you for the rest of your life in a way that feels meaningful to you.

Find your support system

Try to make sure you have a support system in place. If you are supporting other people after the death of your child, such as your partner or other children and family members, it is important that you also take time to talk about and share your grief. You cannot pour from an empty cup; if you are to help others, you must first be strong enough to look after yourself. Ask a good friend to help with your post or emails for a while and ask another to do your shopping. Giving friends specific jobs allows them to feel like they are helping and gives you the space you need to stay more able to help everyone else.

Be honest about your capacity

Often, other people don't understand how exhausting grief can be. If you are seeing other people, it can help to give them a time frame that reflects your ability to cope with company and talking (tip: it's usually never more than one cuppa and an hour).

Tackle holidays and traditions before they tackle you

Take ownership of the times you know will be difficult, such as the lead-up to religious holidays, your child's birthday and the summer holidays. When an adult child dies, there are usually many years' worth of memories and traditions that they will no longer be here for. Every family has its traditions: grandfathers who dress up as Santa; mums or dads who make a special recipe every year for religious or cultural celebrations; holidays in the same place every year with family friends. Whatever they are, the death of an adult child casts a long shadow over these family occasions and they are missed for all the specialness they brought to them. Nothing can ever be the same. Taking time beforehand to prepare can make all the difference. If you are staying somewhere for a special occasion, such as Christmas, take a candle to light at the table for your child or a decoration you can hang on the tree in their name. This also invites others to talk about your child when they might otherwise think it is best to avoid the subject.

Consider going away

Some parents choose to go away for the festive period or at other significant times. This can be a good thing to do as it creates new memories for you, but it is also important to anticipate how you might feel about being so far away from where your child is buried or their ashes are kept or scattered. It can feel like an act of abandonment so be sure to consider how you will feel about being away before you book anything. Grief travels with you wherever you go.

Write to your child

A popular loss-oriented behaviour for parents in grief is to write to their child. This is especially comforting for parents who are missing an older or adult child with whom they might have had regular 'grown-up' conversations. It could be a daily letter or a weekly diary, or simply a folder of scribbles and notes. It doesn't matter how it looks and it doesn't need to be something you show to other people. It is about the process of writing itself; getting all of your thoughts out onto the page and, in doing so, feeling connected to your child. Tell your child about your life, their siblings, their child or children, if they had them, and reflect on things that are happening in the world or within your area that you think might interest them. These letters and journals are a record of your feelings in grief over the months and years after your child has died. In this sense, it is some of the most important grief work there is and you should never imagine that it is a silly or pointless activity. Bereaved parents have taught me that it is hugely helpful to many of them.

Dare to live again

Part of being more restorative in grief is to dare to enjoy life and to live again. There is no upside in the death of a child at any age, but the parents of adults who have died have usually been able to establish a more independent life since the years when their child was young. Hobbies, friends, careers and much-loved pets have all become important, and they can be a lifeline when your adult child dies. Try not to let these things disappear from your life when grief arrives or to feel that you no longer deserve them. The joy a new puppy or kitten can bring or the thrill of mastering a new hobby or skill will help you to live the rest of your life as fully as you can.

To grieve for an older child is to grieve for someone whose life has been entwined with your own for many years. Adjusting to a world without them is not only about missing them and longing for them to be here, but about redefining yourself and learning to live with a lifetime of memories behind you. Bereaved parents and the wider families of older children have shown me there is a life ahead in which these memories can eventually become a source of great comfort and pride, and the life you have shared together undiminished by their death.

Tom Love was a young man who died aged 21 in 2022, while living and working in the Democratic Republic of the Congo as part of a trip through Africa on his motorbike. While there, he contracted an infectious disease which went undiagnosed before it was too late and he died shortly before meeting up with his family and girlfriend Jasmine for Christmas in South Africa. Jasmine writes:

> 'I still have some desperately sad times, where I feel angry and alone, but I also feel now a lot of happiness and joy and gratefulness. There is not a straight road to grief, only ups and downs, and I have found that a great support system can help you weather through both.
>
> 'The most comforting phrase I have found through this whole ordeal is that grief is the price we pay for love, that there is not loss without love. And I know I loved Tom very deeply and that's why I miss him so greatly.'

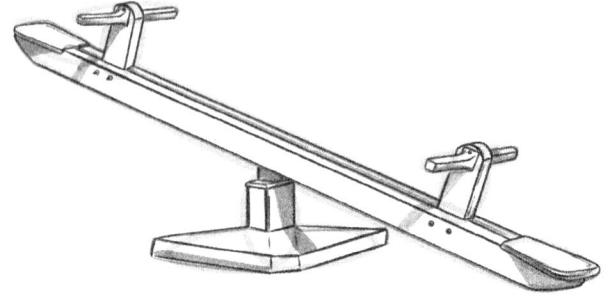

Chapter 6

Managing the Parent Relationship

'The death of our son put our relationship to the test. It has been tested in every possible way and we have come out with a very particular bond, built on love and catastrophe.'

Nick Cave, *El País*, 8 September 2024

What constitutes a family today, what makes a parent a parent, a mother a mother or a father a father? As I write this book in 2025, these questions are becoming harder to answer, or perhaps it is that they are becoming more meaningless and unnecessary to ask at all. In the years that I have been supporting bereaved parents, gender, sexual orientation, attitudes to marriage and single parenting, and what all of these things mean in our grief when a child dies, have undergone enormous transformations. Many of the ideas about the roles and needs of grieving mothers and fathers that pervaded when I first began working with bereaved parents now seem rather archaic.

For example, back then, it was nearly always the case that, when a child died, especially in a hospital, their mother was considered to be the chief mourner. While a mother was expected by the professionals, like doctors and nurses, and others around them to cry and show distress (and was often treated as having psychiatric needs should her distress begin to feel too uncomfortable for others), the father was expected to be strong. He was usually given the 'work' to do of informing relatives and registering the death; he was pushed to the edges of the experience and expected to do his crying in private. He was also expected to return to his work quite soon afterwards. Mothers, while not always treated as sensitively as they could have been, were usually expected to be more deeply affected by their child's death and, because it was less common for women to have careers, many would do their grieving in isolation at home, or in the company of their other children and family.

Nearly all of the parental relationships I encountered back then were heterosexual and parents tended to be married, at least for appearance's sake. Babies and children raised by so-called unmarried women, same-sex parents of any gender and women using fertility treatments by choice with donor sperm were still rare.

Thankfully, time has seen the idea of a family evolve and today the story is very different: in my work, I meet and support families of all shapes and sizes, people whose stories rarely conform to the now-outdated norm. Same-sex parents, single parents and single parents by choice are a small but increasing part of my work, and I am always grateful to those parents who show me the way when breaking down barriers and challenging stereotypes.

This does not mean, however, that the old expectations of what parents, women and men, should and shouldn't do in grief don't still linger on, as they do in almost every aspect of life. Even the most modern father can find himself automatically assuming the 'strong' role of the caretaker in grief, going back to work and perhaps remaining rather detached to keep the ship steady. And even the most independent, self-supporting mother can find herself feeling entirely helpless and vulnerable in her grief. Couples, heterosexual, same-sex and non-binary, may also find themselves having expectations of each other and how the other one should or shouldn't behave in their grief, as can their wider families, support networks and society at large. Medical professionals, doctors, nurses and even grief counsellors can all still carry preconceived notions about how men and women should and shouldn't behave in grief. Much has changed, but change is an ongoing process. So it is against this backdrop of scattering stereotypes that I share with you my learnings from parents, my thoughts and experiences on the different behaviours of mothers and fathers, together and apart, cisgender and LGBTQIA+, indeed anyone with parental responsibility, who is mourning the death of a much-loved child.

The Parent Relationship in Grief

The partnership of two people whose child has died faces enormous challenges, both in the early stages of grief and throughout the years to come. Whether their child is a newborn baby, a toddler, an independent teenager or a young adult who has left home, most parenting couples have been largely focused on creating and raising that child together, so that there now can be a vast space, one that is both physical and emotional, at the heart of their relationship. Staring into this void, with none of the day-to-day duties their child once offered them to distract them from one another, is a frightening prospect for any relationship, no matter how deep and strong the foundations might be. The presence of other children may lessen the void, but doesn't ever fill it.

In the early hours, days and weeks of their grief, it is common for many couples to feel united, and to need to be close to one another. Only the other parent knows their child as intimately and in such detail, so their partner represents the most vital link they have to the child who has died. Only our partner understands the way we have hoped for our child and experienced becoming their parent, what it has meant to us and how we have felt through all of the ups and downs. They have seen us and been with us and our child at our lowest and most vulnerable moments and have witnessed our greatest joys.

Time can stand still for couples not only in the days immediately following their child's death, but also in the weeks after. A journey home from the hospital with an empty car seat or a first night at home knowing the house will never be the same again can feel like out-of-body experiences, and many couples find they don't want to let each other out of their sight in these early days. It is only as time begins to pass and 'normal' life starts to seep in at the edges of their shock, that many couples can find themselves feeling a new distance between them. (If one or both parents have witnessed their child's shock death they can also be traumatised and find it difficult to even begin to talk about what has happened, let alone to think of each other and their relationship. If there is this kind of trauma, it needs to be addressed and worked with by a qualified professional. See page 41 for more on traumatic grief.)

This change in the relationship often begins when one parent goes back to work. Historically, this was the father as he was usually the breadwinner, but, in today's world, that isn't always the case and many women and same-sex partners are the main breadwinners. Whichever parent it is, someone needs to return to work as there is usually a home to pay for and sometimes other children to support. Many corporate policies on bereavement are still woefully inadequate and offer little flexibility for parents. And for the self-employed, there is no choice but to get back to work. Although it is not necessarily anyone's choice, this simple act of leaving the home (or even simply stepping out of home life to the virtual office) and focusing on something else can be restorative and a welcome opportunity to focus on something else for the person who is stepping out. Conversely, this apparent return to some kind of normality, and the physical act of leaving the home where grief now lives, can appear to the other parent as cold and abandoning. They might feel more comfortable at home among their child's belongings, close to where they still feel their child's presence, and feel surprised that their partner can bring themselves to leave, even if their rational brain tells them it is necessary.

In Chapter 1 I described the dual process of grief (see page 21) and this model becomes especially pertinent when offering grief support to couples. As a reminder, the dual process suggests that anyone who is grieving tends to engage in two kinds of behaviour. One is restorative, such as getting back to work, keeping busy with jobs at home or forging ahead with new projects, while the other is loss, such as the need to talk about what's happened over and over again, crying and sharing painful feelings or simply choosing to stay at home and not necessarily mixing with other people. Both types of behaviour are normal, valid and important to the grieving process, and most parents will slip between both ways of being at one point or another. But often, one parent leans more naturally towards the restorative side of their process and appears to be more busy and able to reintegrate with the world, while the other remains in loss and, in doing so, seems unable to 'get back' to a normal life. In my experience, it is when partners fail to understand and validate each other's restorative and loss behaviours that problems can arise.

As a counsellor, I usually get the first request for help from the parent who is feeling more restorative in their grief. Again, historically, this has tended to be a worried father who believes his partner is so tearful she might be losing her mind, she might appear to be wallowing and isolating herself or seems unable to 'pull herself together'. A grieving mother who cannot be reached can be frightening for their partner, who worries she may never return to her old self. But it can sometimes be the other way around, and it is a mother who feels her partner is not coping well. If she is accustomed to keeping her emotions private, she may find any display of emotion from her partner uncomfortable and irritating. In same-sex partnerships, it can be either partner who makes the call. In truth, it doesn't matter which parent or gender is being this or that, the important thing is that, when two parents are occupying entirely different ends of the spectrum, it is hard for them both to feel connected – and the longer they stay there looking at each other from so far away, the harder it becomes for them to reach one another.

When I suggest that they come along to our sessions together, there may be a little resistance – because one partner is accustomed to getting on with things, going back to work and being the pillar of strength for the family, they imagine they do not need any help. I explain that it is very helpful for both parents to come along together if at all possible, even if it is only for the first session, because invariably the communication we share is helpful and makes them feel closer. There is no right way to be, nothing is wrong with the way either parent is responding, and often it is the lack of understanding about the way a partner is behaving in their grief that causes the greatest problems for couples when their child has died.

Roger was a long-distance lorry driver who called me to ask if I would talk to his wife, Sheila. They had three children, but the eldest had died a few months ago. Sheila looked after the two younger children when Roger was at work. Roger complained that it had been a while since their eldest child had died now and his wife was still crying whenever he got home at night. She'd stopped cooking dinner for him and found the other children were a lot of work for her on her own. Sometimes they weren't dressed or washed when he got back, and Sheila was letting them run wild. Roger had no idea what was wrong with her or what to do. He was away for many hours each day and was unfamiliar with the woman he came home to. Sheila, in turn, felt that he didn't care about their dead daughter as he never mentioned her. When I asked Roger, with encouragement, to share his thoughts about his little daughter Holly, Roger said he missed her very much and said some nights it was so bad that, on his way home, he'd drive his lorry up to the cemetery gates and, if he positioned the lorry lights towards Holly's grave, he could flicker a message to her. Sheila was silent, but went across to Roger and put her arms around him, saying: 'I didn't know you felt like that; why haven't you told me?' It was a bittersweet moment for her that he cared so much after all.

The seesaw of grief

When parents are struggling with their grief, I imagine them on a seesaw – one is down at the heavy end, full of loss feelings, and the other is on the lighter end being restorative and getting on with life. When a couple are in that tilted position, they are often unable to move closer to each other and seesaw together. The difficulty appears to be that the person on the heavy end is unable to get up, to function very well after the loss of a child, while their partner appears to manage and seldom says anything about their grief feelings. The partner on the lighter end wants life to get back to normal.

Most often, it is the parent at the heavy end of the seesaw who wants to talk more about their feelings and their child. If I tell them about a local support group or someone they might find comforting to meet, they are often more enthusiastic about this than the parent at the lighter end of the seesaw. Meanwhile, the other parent tends to find the thought of talking any more than is necessary about their dead child uncomfortable and sees this kind of thing as something that will create even more sadness and prefers to keep their emotions private. A parent who is deep in the throes of their loss behaviour can be worrisome to their restorative partner, who thinks their partner is somehow losing control or even that they may leave them. How will they ever get the seesaw moving again? Meanwhile, the parent at the bottom finds their partner distant and business-like and rigid in their efforts to restore normality; they may even feel they do not care or have not loved their child as much as they have. It's not that either parent feels more or less, or is doing it wrong or right; they are simply expressing and experiencing their grief differently.

Of course, rare is the parent who does not care, or one who cares too much, or one who cares in the wrong way. They are all simply facets of grief, catching the light and shade of their new reality in different ways and from different angles. We all bring our unique way of grieving to the death of a child. How you react is always based on your life experiences and the values you were raised with. Our parents may have encouraged us to keep a stiff upper lip in times of trouble, or dismissed any high emotions as weakness. We may have lived with parents whose own emotional boundaries were weak or non-existent and so have come to expect to be relied upon by others, or else overwhelmed by other people's emotions. We may have already seen our siblings or parents die, or death may never have crossed our paths until now. There is no technical drawing, no instructions for use, about the way two parents might experience their own child's death.

The important thing in supporting grieving parents is not particularly where these different responses come from, or indeed who is on which end of the seesaw, but instead how to bring them closer together and get the seesaw moving – to put a little more weight on the high end and take a little of the load off the lower one. Because when they come closer together, even just ever so slightly, there is a shift towards greater balance and a feeling of greater emotional closeness for both parents.

For some couples, this might be a simple process of openly sharing and listening to each other's feelings. For others, this can be a long and painful process, peeling back layers of generational pain and problems. All of our life experiences are part of how we react to every situation and it is always helpful to talk to your partner about the difficult times and endings of any sort that they may have experienced as a child or younger adult. The more understanding of a partner's own background and experience there is, the easier it is to accept and, if necessary, forgive their behaviours if they are at odds with our own. What's certain is that the death of a child rarely diminishes any existing issues within the relationship; instead, it lays everything bare. Issues around in-laws or siblings, and pre-existing grudges and disputes all rear their heads higher and with greater force than ever before. Whatever the process involves, both must be willing to open their eyes a little wider and see the pain they are experiencing through their partner's eyes.

The Issue of Blame

Sometimes when a child dies, they have been in the care of one of their parents and not the other. Even though the child's death is a tragic accident or the result of an unforeseen event or medical condition (for example, a baby who unexpectedly stops breathing), the parent who is 'on duty' when the child dies will naturally feel more responsible for what has happened. This is understandable and entirely human. We all feel responsible when something bad happens on our watch, whatever it might be. But when what happens is the worst thing imaginable for any parent, it can have a profound impact on the parents' relationship and almost always brings further complexity to the feelings experienced by both parents after their child's death. There is greater shame, remorse and torturous guilt for one; for the other, confusion, resentment and sometimes a deep but often unexpressed natural anger towards their partner. One parent can never forgive themselves, while the other wants to and does forgive their partner, but their forgiveness can never quite be accepted. And somewhere among it all there is a great love, pity and sorrow for each other and the pain they are experiencing together. It takes a huge amount of commitment, care and trust for the relationship to survive and continue.

Sometimes when there is an issue of apparent blame, the parent who considers themselves to be responsible finds it easier to stay close to the pain, to reject any hope of forgiveness. Self-punishing behaviours such as isolating, not eating, substance abuse and other forms of self-harm can emerge and it can be extremely worrying for those around them to witness.

It is important for both parents to get help for themselves and together. This may be through the NHS or a charity experienced in providing the necessary grief counselling support. Supporting a couple who are grieving for their child requires specific skills and experience and you should always make sure you are seeing a counsellor who is appropriately trained and supervised. (See page 51 for advice on finding a bereavement counsellor.)

Accepting that you cannot change the events that happened when your child died is one of the kindest things you can do for your partner and your relationship. It can at times feel like a hopeless situation, but the quiet, simple consistency of a partner's support, even if it is unspoken, is a powerful comfort.

Single Parents and Blended Families

Not all parents are married or in a relationship when their child dies. Divorced and separated parents who might have existing grievances and those with new partners and half-siblings of the child who has died can all bring unique perspectives and challenges to this experience.

If the child's death occurred while one parent was with them or if there is existing animosity of any kind, as there often is after a divorce, there is enormous potential for additional emotional pain. Parents can feel the need to 'protect' their child's funeral and other events from new partners and stepfamilies, who they may feel are not welcome to share in the grief of the child's family of origin. Everything divorced and separated parents are dealing with is amplified with the death of a child and an enormous amount of emotional maturity is required, at exactly the moment when many of us feel exposed and almost childlike ourselves.

If it is at all possible to find a way to work together, family counselling can be extremely helpful for everyone in working through this difficult situation, especially if there are other children and partners involved. The guidance of an experienced counsellor who understands your complex struggles can help you to empathise with each other's needs and move towards creating stronger bonds that can benefit you and others in your family network.

Making a Relationship Work After the Death of a Child: Some Things You Might Find Useful

The death of a child sharply pulls parents from their everyday lives and forces them to rethink and re-evaluate everything they knew before. Relationships that once felt solid can begin to crack, as the effects of your grief take hold. Understanding and forgiving one another will help you through the difficult times.

Keep talking and sharing

It can be helpful to talk about your child with each other, use their name and keep them present in your home, especially if you have other children.

Ask each other when the time is right how they have felt that day. It is always OK to ask and to say something – never avoid talking about your feelings or your child for fear of upsetting your partner. And if talking feels too hard, find other ways to share your feelings – a walk and a talk together is often helpful. A father who rarely shared his grief brought home a painting he'd found in a charity shop of a young girl. He had it framed because he said he thought the girl in it looked how his daughter might have looked if she'd had the chance to grow older. This simple and thoughtful gesture helped his wife, who was so pleased to hear and see how he felt and was touched by this simple gesture. Keeping silent, or not doing something, for fear of upsetting your partner is how chasms grow between people.

Plan a date to share

Stepping into and understanding the way your partner is feeling their grief is perhaps the most powerful and effective way to help both of you accept and embrace each other's often puzzling behaviours. Rather than accusing your partner of not caring enough or of wallowing in their despair, try to be curious about the way they are coping instead. A 'grief date' lets you inhabit their mindset for a period of time – it could be an hour or a day – to further understand the choices they are making and the way they are behaving. It's not about trying to convince yourself to be more like them, or them like you, but about increasing awareness on both sides and getting the seesaw we talked about earlier moving.

Turn to your community and friends

Time and again, I have seen how community can wrap around a couple grieving the death of a child. While many grieving couples may not wish to see people or be engaged in any social activities, simply knowing that their local community is thinking about them can be incredibly supportive to them as individuals and to the relationship. Taking away the pressure of domestic duties by cooking a meal or inviting other children to play dates, and showing support in other ways, such as lighting candles in a church or raising money for a cause that affects them, can all help a couple feel held by their community. If your community is not a geographical one but is instead a team or a workplace, this can be equally comforting, and I encourage you to try to accept the offers of help and sympathy that will inevitably come your way.

Plan for special occasions and milestones

While every day is difficult, some days, such as birthdays, religious holidays, anniversaries and events like what would have been their first day of school or a return to university, can carry extra pain and leave you feeling heightened sensitivity to events and the people around you. Try to plan for these inevitable moments and reassure each other that you are facing them together. For example, on special occasions, you might choose to light a big candle and tell everyone at the table that the candle represents your child, so that they are not forgotten. If a birthday is coming up, make plans to spend the day together doing something you both find helpful.

Maintain physical contact

Sex and lovemaking are often at the heart of what many couples struggle with in grief. One partner may find having sex very comforting, almost necessary, as a way of releasing pent-up emotion and experiencing closeness when words fail them. Others find that sex is almost too much to bear – it can feel invasive and too tender, and open the floodgates of emotions when they are already overflowing. One partner might make advances and the other might reject them, and the whole thing can create an even greater void than is already in place. What nearly all couples can agree on is that warm, caring physical contact such as hugging, holding hands, massage and other forms of touch that don't automatically provide a gateway to sex are always comforting and welcome. The important thing is to establish what you are both comfortable with and want. If you would like to be held but do not wish for a hug to lead to anything else more sexual, that is perfectly understandable, but it can be helpful to be clear to your partner that is all that you can cope with for now. Do not feel you need to please anyone and, equally, do not feel ashamed about asking for physical closeness. The key, as always, is to talk to your partner.

Go where you find the greatest comfort

Some friends and family members might be very difficult for you or your partner to be around so try not to feel any pressure to see or spend time with them. Some people will pop by and invite you to things with the best intentions and you may not wish to accept their offer. Taking a moment to discuss with each other who and what might be problematic for you both can help you feel that you are working together and protecting your space and grief.

Similarly, seek out the environments and places that make you both feel at ease. Whether it is walking in the countryside, going to the pub for lunch or being at home together, being yourselves in places where you feel authentic and at ease with one another can be enormously helpful to you both.

Look after yourself

> 'I can do nothing for you but work on myself … you can do nothing for me but work on yourself!'
>
> **Ram Dass,** *Be Here Now*

The kindest and most helpful thing you can do for your partner in grief is to look after yourself. This does not mean you shouldn't lean on them when you need them or feel able to ask for more support sometimes. It means acknowledging that there is no remedy for your pain and that your partner cannot be the person to heal you. Once you remove this expectation from your relationship, you can get on with the business of mourning alongside the one person in the world who loves your child as much as you do.

There is no greater challenge to a relationship than the death of a much-loved child, whatever their age. Some couples find that they begin to fall apart without the glue of their child to hold them together. However, many find the experience they share in their grief creates a new and lasting bond between them – one that can never be broken.

As Mark Guinn, father of Hazel who died aged three in 2003, says:

> 'We feel we might be better people for what we have been through, although we wish we hadn't. We batten down the hatches quite often at home; people may ring and try to make contact sometimes but we just want us. You know what you have got then.'

Chapter 7

Supporting Your Children When a Sibling Dies

'If you have a sister and she dies, do you stop saying you have one? Or are you always a sister, even when the other half of the equation is gone?'

Jodi Picoult, *My Sister's Keeper*

The death of a child is always a terrible shock to everyone in their family and, if the child has siblings, this is especially true for them. The impact of this life-changing event will naturally depend on how closely they were involved in each other's daily lives, the circumstances of the child's death and the ages of their siblings. For some, especially those who are physically close in age and have spent their childhoods together, the death of a sibling leaves an enormous gap and can create a kaleidoscope of changing emotions throughout their lives. For others who did not get to know their sibling well, there can be a wistful fascination and a yearning for the brother or sister they never had the chance to know. Some children can feel a sense of rivalry with the dead child, who now occupies such a special place in their parents' hearts. Others can find themselves strongly identifying with the dead brother or sister, to the detriment of their relationships with other siblings. However this death impacts them and whatever the circumstances, most bereaved siblings will know and feel throughout their own lives that someone significant to them in their family is sadly missing.

When a sibling dies, their death brings with it a very real understanding that they too can die and that anyone they love and depend upon can also die at any time. Their mortality is brought into sharp focus and their own identity forever changed. A third-born child will never be one of three again and miss being the baby of the family. A twin or triplet will no longer be reflected by their other sibling, and no longer feel part of a special duo or trio. A second-in-line may now need to take on the responsibilities previously borne by their older sibling and yet not ever feel ready for such a role. However and wherever the tear is made, it will stay there forever and is likely to create many other tiny rips and tears in the lives of bereaved siblings over the years that follow.

Parents who are grieving deeply themselves may need additional support and guidance when supporting their children. Careful, considerate handling and an awareness of what to expect when children are grieving, as well as patience in the face of the challenging behaviour that almost certainly lies ahead, will help parents to manage this often overlooked aspect of grief when a child dies.

Telling Siblings What Has Happened

The way you tell your child or children is an important element of the story of their sibling's death that they will carry with them in their minds throughout their lives. Your family culture and belief systems will influence the way you approach telling your child or children and, for many families, the traditions and practices of their faith may provide great comfort and guidance in this. So, too, will any previous experience of death if the family has had any, perhaps after the death of a grandparent or a much-loved pet, for example. Whatever your cultural background or religious faith, and even if your child has known for some time that their sibling is not expected to live, it will always be a shock. To understand that they really have died will mean they are likely to experience many new and varied feelings they have not felt before.

For this reason, it is always a good idea to give some serious thought to the way you are going to tell your child or children, and prepare them gently for what you are going to say.

Young children

If you are telling a young child that their sibling has died, it is usually best to be somewhere familiar and quiet, where they can feel comfortable. Sit together and explain slowly that you have some very sad news to tell them.

When you are telling your child about their sibling's death, keep in mind that they may think, as many young children do, that people only die when they are old. It can help them to understand death if you explain that when we die, our bodies do not work anymore. It is usually best to avoid focusing too much on a particular part of the body that has stopped working, for example their sibling's heart, as this may then become a part of their body they feel anxious about. It can also be reassuring for them to know that their sibling is not in any pain and can no longer feel things or see or hear.

Some parents might be tempted to try to preserve their child's innocence and may avoid using honest, truthful language; to talk of siblings having 'passed away' or 'to be with Granddad', or any kind of alternative to the facts – that they have died – that makes their death seem less painful and real.

While rooted in good intentions, this can be confusing and unhelpful for children in the long run. Creating a fairy tale around their sibling's death or describing it in terms of make-believe or magic might feel like a kind thing to do, but psychologists now agree that parents need to be honest and as clear as they can be, using simple language that their children will easily understand. This is so that children are left with no room for doubt or misinterpretation of the events, both now and in the future.

Using simple, age-appropriate language means that there will be less confusion in their minds. It can be extremely hard and daunting to say such words as *dead* and *died* to a young child, but bereaved parents have taught me that, in the end, it is the most helpful way when having what is undoubtedly one of the hardest conversations any parent can ever have. No matter how clear you are, you may find that your child or children will ask you about what has happened again and again; they are just trying to make sense of what they have been told.

Nikki, who we met in earlier chapters, recalls telling her son, Adam, about his sister Rosie's death on the day she died:

> 'Adam had been there that morning; he was four and a half years old. We'll never forget the evening we had to sit and break the devastating news to him. Like all young brothers and sisters, they had been

two peas in a pod, always together, and that was the only world he knew. As adults, it felt impossible for us to process a sudden loss without any explanation, so we had no idea how to help our son do this. This confusion was coupled with a paralysing fear of whether we or our son were also at risk of dying suddenly.

'I remember lying in bed and Adam repeatedly asking "but why did she die?" I tried my best to answer and console him, but the words sounded useless and inherently wrong. "We don't know darling. Her body stopped working and that hardly ever happens. Rosie was just super unlucky and that is really sad."

'He would sometimes ask if he would die like Rose did. I'd answer: "No sweetheart. Because Rosie died, we have been given extra check-ups that she didn't have. They mean we are all safe." I was able to do this because we had cardiac screening as a family. This was reassuring, but I knew I was only giving him half the truth. We had screening that was negative for any conditions, but we still had no answers about why she had died – maybe it was nothing to do with the heart. Anxiety about Adam and my other, subsequent children has felt all-consuming at times. But I have learned how to cope with this.'

Many children will have other questions about their sibling's death and often parents don't know the answers yet. If you don't know the answers to their questions, it is OK to explain to your child that you don't know yet and to reassure them that you will tell them as soon as you know. When you lack answers to some of their questions, it can be helpful to tell your child what you do know, not only about their sibling's death, but about the way the days and weeks ahead will go. Remind and reassure them of the things they can be certain of – for example, name all the people in your family who you will tell and who will be around them, and even tell them when normal things like teatime will happen and mention pets and other sources of comfort like friends and school. If your child has never attended one or been told about funerals, it can be helpful to explain to them why we have them and how they can help us to say goodbye. You can explain about where a funeral is held and the use of flowers and the rituals of your faith if you have one, why some families donate to charities, who a celebrant or what a wake is or indeed anything else about the days and weeks to come that might feel new and unfamiliar to them. It might sound obvious, but, at a time when life feels so uncertain, it can be very reassuring for your child to know about what is steady and sure.

There may be sadness and tears and it is important to reassure young children that this is natural and understandable. It can also be important to encourage young children to have a fun time and play with whatever makes them happy, and to let them know they can still play their favourite game or watch their favourite television programme if they want to after you have told them. Young children are unlikely to sit with upset feelings for long; they may express themselves only in short outbursts and often these may not be obviously related to the death of their sibling. A little boy's three-year-old sister died and, when he was told, he burst into tears and was very upset. As his father picked him up and hugged him, he spotted his sister's bike in the corner of the room and immediately jumped down, asking, 'Can I have her bike now?' This didn't mean he wasn't still upset. Children can easily switch from being very sad to being very playful and happy; this is natural and is the way they manage their grief. Many parents will want to sit and cuddle their children and feel close to them, and this is understandable, but young children will naturally want to play and carry on with whatever games they are interested in. It can help to understand that our need to be close to our living young children is natural, but it is unlikely that they will be able to provide us with the comfort we need.

There can also sometimes be a temptation to tell younger children about their sibling's death 'in a while' or a bit later on. Many parents imagine that if they can just have a bit of time to gather their thoughts and feelings or understand more about what has happened themselves, they will be better equipped to tell their other child or children. Often the minutes and hours after a child dies are busy ones for parents, with doctors and hospitals or else police or other services to deal with. It can be necessary to ask a grandparent or friend to look after your child or children for a while as you deal with everything. Let the person who is looking after them know that your child or children don't know about the death yet, and keep in mind that it is usually best that you find the moment and tell the children as soon as you can about what has happened. With the passing of time, there is too much opportunity for them to overhear conversations, develop suspicions or stumble upon the truth themselves in an unhelpful way.

Although it can feel daunting to talk to young children in such honest terms and use words like dying and died, in years to come they will know that you told them the truth and that you can be trusted, and that they were an important person to you in this moment.

Older children

Teenagers and older children are usually more able to understand death in adult terms, so it is unlikely you'll need to explain to them what dead means, but they will still need to be told factually and kindly about their sibling's death in the same straightforward and honest language so that they feel they are trusted with important information and do not create their own stories.

All teenagers are different, but they are also universal in that they are all going through enormous physical and emotional changes, and the death of a sibling adds to the already heavy burden they carry but often do not want to share. Their independence and private worlds are incredibly important to them and the death of a sibling can seem like an unwelcome inconvenience as well as a robbery of their identity and the fun they were expecting to be able to have at this time of their own life. Their need for independence can also get in the way of being able to accept the love and support they need at this time. It is important, when telling older children or teens, that you acknowledge how this death will affect them, and empathise with their point of view. Allow them the space they need, but reassure them that they are not alone and you are here for them when they need you.

Some older children and teenagers might feel comfortable with physical affection and comfort from their parents, but, for many, it is awkward and to be avoided at all costs. This is often the case and there is no need to force hugs or physical closeness if they do not want it, even if they are visibly upset. Many parents find going for a walk or a drive, where their teenagers are not required to make eye contact or talk directly to them, can be a good time to communicate.

A mum told me how much it meant to her when her teenage son hugged her while she was washing up after dinner and quietly sobbing. He had seemed uninterested in his younger sister's death, but, on this evening, without being prompted, he hugged his mum while her hands were safely in the sink and he didn't have to look directly at her.

Reassure them that it is okay to have their own space and private time with or without you. Although they may be extremely articulate and confident, many teenagers will feel scared of what the future holds for them now and worried about their own life, and about you as their grieving parent or parents, although they may not be able to say so. Anxiety in loss if often not recognised and yet it is one of the most significant feelings associated with grief. It can also help you to accept that it is likely your teenager will have times when they are angry and non-communicative about their sibling's death. Parents are most helpful when they can accept this and don't try to force conversations. Simply reassure them that however they feel is fine and that their feelings are just that; it is only ever what they choose to do with them that can be good or bad.

It is seldom helpful to ask a young person how they feel, but it can be very helpful to share with them how you are feeling, without expecting them to tell you how they feel in response. Whether you are angry about a late diagnosis or having to do all the planning for the funeral or cross with a relative for the way they have behaved, saying it out loud may just help them to identify their own emotions and feelings, and may reassure them that it's OK for them to have guilty or angry feelings too. They will naturally be curious about the way you are responding and may look to you for guidance with their feelings and behaviour. They will appreciate that you are sharing your feelings with them and will almost certainly be able to relate to them, even if they don't tell you so. Some young people (especially, although not exclusively, boys) might not say anything at all about the sibling who has died and this can be very worrying and excluding for parents. It can be tempting to try to push children into talking and sharing their feelings, but often this can instead push them away. Although we might find it very concerning when our older children don't talk to us, it is usually best to let them find their own time and space to do so. This can be an extra burden for grieving parents to carry, but try to trust that they almost certainly will find a friend to confide in and talk to.

Whatever their age, many children can worry that they have somehow played a part in causing this dreadful thing to happen to their sibling, perhaps by having bad thoughts about them or saying something mean to them before they died. Sibling rivalry is natural and happens between most brothers and sisters, and is often behind the guilt many children have when a sibling dies. For parents, grandparents or other family members, it can be helpful to show you are interested in a bereaved young person who might be feeling this way and to listen to how they feel without any criticism or judgement. Reassure your child that most children have fought with their siblings and feel angry about things they have said or done, and experience regret, but this does not mean they have played a part in their sibling's death in any way, or that they didn't love them. The most helpful thing parents can do is to be non-judgemental – try not to give advice but instead show how much you rate and love them with lots of kind gestures and uplifting words. If they had quarrelled or fallen out with their sibling beforehand, it may take time for them to tell you about this. Do try to stress that their behaviour does not affect the facts of their death. As always, talking about these things as calmly as possible keeps the door open, as does doing things together like cooking and shopping for ingredients to cook together. These gentle, collaborative activities give young people the chance to share their feelings without pressure and can help to make their load lighter to carry.

Children's Responses

There is no right way for children to respond when they are told a sibling has died, although most will burst into tears and then want to know why and how. However old they are when it happens, it is an early lesson in the fragility of their own life, and of those they love, that is likely to create ripples in their mood and behaviour for some time, if not a lifetime.

Many children will cry and want physical comfort, but just as many will wish to be left alone to process the information in their own way. Every child reacts differently, both in the early days of their understanding of their sibling's death and as time passes. An important thing to remember is that no child's response is wrong or something you need to worry about (unless it hurts them or someone else). It is not unusual for some children to smile or even giggle when hearing the news. They're not being rude or cruel; laughter is a way of displacing their emotions when they feel too overwhelmed, and can sometimes be a way to hide their discomfort.

Some children can find that the news that a sibling has died embarrasses them, as does all the attention and fuss of people coming to the house and asking how they are. A young girl whose brother died refused to go to the school they both attended one morning because of all the flowers that had been left outside the school gates. She didn't want to be in the limelight over her brother's death, associated with his death or receive so much unwelcome attention from her friends, teachers or parents. Children seldom want to be different and a child dying in the family is very different, and siblings will need to manage this big change in their lives.

Some children become very curious about the death and what happened, especially if their sibling died when they were still a baby. Some children find themselves wanting to identify very closely with a sibling who died before they were born, more so at times than with any living siblings. Children may feel an affinity with the sibling who has died, especially if they feel frustrated by other brothers or sisters, or want to identify themselves with the familial characteristics of their sibling who has died, and this can last well into their adulthood.

For others, there is a sense of rivalry with the dead child, who in their death can be perceived as their parents' favourite or as being very special. A dead child can never leave their room in a mess or receive a disappointing school report and, in this sense, their siblings can come to resent them for their perceived perfection.

Another reaction, regardless of age, is for siblings to feel anger – anger for being robbed of their sibling and anger generally at the world, for all the changes that bereavement brings. Some children also feel angry towards their dead sibling, for spoiling life and everything at home. Feeling angry is not unusual – it is as usual as sadness, although often it is not recognised and often downplayed or frowned upon. If you are managing an overtly angry child or one who hides their anger and is silent, try to remain patient and let them work through their feelings. Most children respond well to physical exercise or doing things together with a parent, and this can lessen their anxiety. Anger is most often an expression of deeper underlying feelings in grief. It is very often linked to the simple and difficult realisation that their sibling will never again be in their life, that their family life has changed forever and that they miss them.

Older children and teenagers who are exploring their own identities and testing their boundaries may well look to the wrong people or behaviours for comfort. It is not unusual for bereaved teens to experiment with drugs, alcohol and other risk-taking behaviours, perhaps more so than their peers. This can be extremely worrying for parents as it can be difficult to manage or even to know about. Communication and maintaining that sense of togetherness in your grief as a family is perhaps the strongest deterrent here. Providing a home where they feel able to be themselves and where their friends feel welcome can also help to keep your teenage children close. Giving them small responsibilities and jobs that they might find rewarding, such as cooking for the family when their friends are visiting, is also a good way to stay connected.

Helping Your Child or Children When Their Sibling Has Died: Some Things You Might Find Useful

It's natural to want to shield children from death, but we now know it's not a healthy way to approach things when a sibling dies. Children of all ages need to be able to say goodbye, and to experience the different feelings grief brings – and when possible to be able to express and explore their grief, just as adults do.

Involve them

It can be so easy to overlook children or believe you are protecting them, but including your child or children in conversations around their sibling's death can be helpful for them. After asking his parents about what happened at a cremation, a ten-year-old boy whose brother died decided he didn't want to go to the funeral service, but instead wanted to stand at the gate with his other brother and hand out the Orders of Service to mourners as they arrived. He felt proud of being at the gates to see everyone as they arrived and that he was at this important event, something he would remember for the rest of his life.

Be mindful of putting children in the limelight

Not all children want the attention that comes with the death of a sibling, especially in the early stages, so be mindful of too much exposure. A young lad told me that when his brother died it was embarrassing because people kept telling him how sorry they were and then ruffling his hair. It's important to involve them, but this doesn't need to mean they are front and centre of everything.

Show them how you feel

Children experiencing grief and death for the first time will be curious to see how you behave and will take their cues from you over the coming weeks and months. There is nothing wrong with showing them your emotions – being sad and angry, and everything else you are feeling, permits them to feel these entirely normal emotions for themselves – though bear in mind that becoming extremely distressed in front of them may be frightening for a child or young person

Acknowledging dates and milestones

Children can understand a lot about how much they are loved by how their parents express their grief when their sibling dies. If parents choose not to tell their other children about a significant anniversary, such as the day their sibling died or their birthday, it is likely that other children will know by their parents' behaviour or mood that something is different today. Explaining the importance of the day and including them in remembering and even celebrating with them in some way, whether through a simple family walk or a pizza with friends, gives children an important message that they too will always be remembered. It can also create an annual ritual that all the family can be part of and ensures the sibling who has died remains part of the family forever.

Keep special items for your living child

They may be too young to be aware yet of special items. Saving something especially for them that belonged to their sibling is a supportive way to provide a physical connection in the future with a special sibling.

Find your child grief support

The death of a sibling may create fears for their brothers and sisters, and some children can develop anxiety around death and dying which can grow and become unhelpful to them as they go on with their lives. Other feelings, of guilt or shame or resentment, can cause problems if they are not acknowledged, recognised and talked about. An educational psychologist covering schools, a school nurse or a bereavement counsellor experienced in working with children will help your child learn to name and manage these difficult feelings and ensure they do not become a burden to them as they grow up. If you are particularly concerned about your child's mental well-being as a result of their bereavement, you may want to find specialist support. Your GP will be able to help you with this.

The healing power of animals

At a time when their whole world has been turned upside down, animals can provide a lot of healing and comfort for bereaved children. It may be your own pet, such as a dog, cat, hamster or rabbit, or one belonging to a friend or relative, or even a friendly donkey at the local city farm. Whatever breed or species they are, animals can give bereaved children a great deal of pure and uncomplicated joy at such a difficult time and a sense of being needed and loved. It is also worth remembering that when a much-loved pet dies it may well bring up feelings of grief about the previous loss of their sibling. Although difficult for them, this is not necessarily a negative experience and very often it teaches children about loss and the feelings loss brings up in us, and how we do manage. It can be a helpful way to express the grief and heartbreak they may not have fully expressed when their sibling died.

Reassure them they can be however they want to be

Children cannot sit with uncomfortable emotions for too long. One of the kindest things a parent can do for their bereaved child is to let them know they can always talk to you, a teacher or someone they trust. This is also true for older children, who need to have all the freedom and fun any child has without fear, guilt or blame.

Building your child's self-esteem

We all need to feel good about ourselves and to have self-esteem about who we are. It is even more important when children experience difficult changes in their lives. Bereaved children need to feel good about themselves in bucketloads. They have been through one of life's hardest things: the loss of a sibling. They need to know that they can manage life and that they can do this now and later in life when hard things inevitably happen.

But self-esteem is not something you can give to children with praise or compliments; self-worth, and the resilience it generates, needs to be something they feel for themselves – it is directly connected to how they feel they are loved and cared about by those around them.

To promote self-esteem and resilience, many therapists will work with bereaved children and their parents using a resilience model developed by the American developmental psychologist Edith Grotberg in 1995. In 'A Guide to promoting resilience in children; strengthening the human spirit' she develops a simple educational concept that many teachers use and it helps children see their own strengths and feel secure about the people who love and care about them.

The resilience model is relevant in families where parents, grandparents and other relatives can interact positively with the bereaved child. It is not something you need to 'do' overtly as a specific exercise or activity – it's more a way of being with your child that you can keep in mind for whenever you talk and spend time with them. It's important that you and the other adults in your family are truthful and congruent with your child, and never say made up things to make them feel better.

1. **I am:** Honestly recognise your child's natural characteristics. This is best done when having an everyday conversation, such as asking about their day at school or with their grandparents. Recognise their characteristics and share with your child what you have noticed about them, for example their kindness or their energy or the way they try hard at school. You can expand on this by telling them they have always been like this and give other examples of this positive attribute. This is about you telling your child what you have noticed about them

with real examples, not asking your child to consider their own attributes. It's also not about their physical features or material possessions, but the very essence of who they are. What makes them the special person who you see?

2. **I have:** Ask your child who the people in their life are, who support and love them no matter what. Then try to expand on this, describing who they are and where they live, for example. All children need to know they have people, whether it is their immediate family, their friends or a kind staff member at school. They may already know who the people are who care about them. Or they may not – sometimes important people, such as grandparents, can live a long way away so it can be comforting to name and identify them. This exercise reminds your child they are not alone and that their family is still their family, even after their sibling has died.

3. **I can:** Everyone needs to feel they can do things and that they are useful. What are the things you see, or perhaps Granny sees, that your child can do? It doesn't need to be something big and impressive; it can be small and simple. The main thing is that they can feel proud of themselves knowing what you and other family members think about it. Examples might include: *I can play football, I can draw funny pictures, I can speak two languages, I can make myself toast.*

Telling a child that their sibling has died is something no parent ever wishes to experience. Honesty is always the best policy, but this doesn't make it any easier to implement at times. As always, talking about and sharing your feelings as a family will help ensure children feel seen and heard in the years that follow their sibling's death. This is not always easy and, in my work supporting families, I have often helped them to create a time, perhaps before dinner on Sunday evenings or whenever works for your family, where everyone can sit around the table and share their thoughts and feelings about their grief and the child they all miss so much.

> 'I feel I know, at a very deep, visceral level, how precious life is and how suddenly it can be taken away. In some ways, sometimes, I almost feel as though I owe it to Clare to live every day as busily and as fully as possible, because she didn't get a chance to live the life I'm living now, with children and a partner and a career and travel and friends and all the things that make adult life interesting and fun.'
>
> **Joanna Moorhead** on her sister, Clare, who died aged three in 1972, in *The Death of a Child* (edited by Peter Stanford)

Chapter 8

Continuing to Parent

He has gone into another room
I cannot find
But I know he was here
Because of all the happiness
He left behind

Ancient Chinese poem, inscribed on the headstone of
Nicky Mountbatten

There is no timeframe or set of stages for your grief when your child dies. Every child and every family is different, as are the circumstances of their death. There will never be a date in the diary that you can look ahead to and know with confidence that, on that day, you will feel better about life or decide that you might want to do something to help other people or create a legacy for your child in the world.

But many parents do find that, over time, they begin to feel that they want to spend time doing things that keep their child close. This can start in the early stages, when parents plan their child's funeral and may tend their grave; these are processes that help parents to make choices for their child and to continue to parent their child. As time passes, most parents want to treasure the memories they have of their child and will eventually find comfort from photographs or painting pictures or making something in their child's name.

After her son's death, Lilli trained as a homeopath and now provides support for bereaved families. She also began to write poetry, inspired by her son, Benny:

An Elephant in the Corner
By Lilli May, 22 February 2008

There's an elephant in the corner.
It's amazing that such a presence
can remain unseen, unfelt,
until you ask 'How many children do you have?'
and I reply 'I had five, but one died last year'.
Then, if you gently ask 'How?'
I will tell you

Benny was a beautiful boy,
twelve years old, full of life,
the middle child of five.
Intelligent, inquisitive, quirky, loving.
A fiddler.

Yes, a great fiddler. He died through his fiddling,
A stupid accident, no one was to blame.

Then maybe you will tell me about your elephant
and a bond will be forged,
or maybe just by acknowledging mine
it will be transformed into the spirit
of a twelve-year-old boy
with sadness, yes, but also joy.

But if all you say is 'I'm sorry'
then change the subject, awkwardly,
the elephant will remain,
a large and uncomfortable presence
too difficult to bear
so we will move away
and you will never know
how the elephant could have changed

into the spirit of a boy.

Whatever parents do, many want to be able to talk about their child, use their name and let other people know how important their child was to them. This is a natural and helpful way of continuing to be a parent after their child has died and can often lead to further activities that also go on to help others.

For some, it is about doing something positive to address an issue that is close to their heart, such as raising money for a charity or lobbying for changes in the law. Others decide to establish new charities and organisations of their own.

There are many ways in which grieving parents approach these projects and initiatives, some of them privately and others outward-facing to the world. Some with small, personal aims and others with huge, world-spanning objectives. No way of approaching this aspect of your grief is better than another and everyone settles on something that feels right to them and their family.

The important thing is not what bereaved parents choose to do, but to acknowledge this as a significant and healing part of parents' grief. In moving forward with a large project or raising money for a small charity with a cake sale, bereaved parents are not somehow moving away from or putting their child behind them. They continue to remember their child in the best way they can. In this way, grieving parents bring their children with them throughout the rest of their lives.

On Faith and Spirituality

Whether they have been raised in a community or family that practices a religious faith or have never been part of or interested in religion, many parents find themselves turning to a faith of some kind after a child dies. Religions differ on the details, but most ultimately teach and believe in a universe where humans are reunited with those we love who have died or else where those we love are reborn. In this sense, faith can provide a space, often shared with others, where parents can feel their child's presence and believe in a world where they will see their child again.

No one can tell you which faith is best or how you should choose your faith, if at all. But bereaved parents have shown me how comforting some of the rituals and beliefs of any faith can be. Even the staunchest atheists can find comfort and reassurance in the words and presence of a local vicar, imam or any kind of religious mentor in their community. These are nearly always compassionate and wise people who know more than most about the pains of death and mourning, and the importance of listening and providing a non-judgemental place where parents can talk about and remember their child.

I once met a father whose six-year-old son was on life support for some weeks as he had decided to donate his son's organs. His organs were going to be sent to various places and, before his life support was turned off, I suggested that the dad might find the support of the hospital chaplain helpful, not because of his beliefs but because he would simply give him space to talk about his son. When I saw the father again, he told me how comforting his meeting with the chaplain had been. The chaplain had asked all about his son and for permission to bless the boy and his father had agreed. The father recounted how reassuring it had been for him, that although he remained an atheist, he was glad his son had been blessed and never regretted the time he had spent with the chaplain.

Many parents talk of feeling their child's presence with them, seeing signs of them in nature and of messages from them through simple things such as birds in the garden or patterns in the clouds. These are all comforting and important to bereaved parents, helping them to feel a connection to their child and a sense that there is a world in which they are still united.

Digging Deep and the Rewards of Gardening for Grief

'To plant a garden is to believe in tomorrow.'

Audrey Hepburn

Bereaved parents I have supported have found a sense of purpose and comfort in gardening and growing. There is something in the idea of nurturing and looking after plants that grow and flourish every year, as well as the physicality of gardening and being outside in the elements, that many parents find helpful. Gardening has proven to be so beneficial for bereaved parents that it has become something I have incorporated into the retreats for bereaved parents that I have run for many years.

For Eleanor, whose daughter Miranda died suddenly and unexpectedly when she was two years old, gardening was the lifeline she needed to carry on:

'Miranda died in January and, by April, I was still in a deep depression. The changing of the seasons, which was usually so welcome, only seemed to remind me that the world was still senselessly turning even though this terrible tragedy had happened.

'One Sunday, my aunt came over and told me we were going to sort out my garden. I had always enjoyed gardening, but I hadn't bothered with it much in recent months. Being outside and hearing the noise of children playing in the park over the road was also unbearable for me at times, and I avoided being out there.

'I had been given two plants when Miranda died: a beautiful yellow Molineux rose and a blueberry bush. We spent the whole day in the garden planting, weeding and pruning, and generally sorting things out.

'That day was the first time that I felt slightly lighter, that I had done something meaningful. I went out again the next day and began to spend more time out there. Being outside, connecting with nature and the life cycle gave me a feeling of peace. It wasn't necessarily something conscious, but by being in the garden I began to feel more connected to Miranda and able to continue to mother her still through all the nurturing and patience and hope that gardening requires.

'Gardening came to mean so much to me that I decided to train in social and therapeutic horti-culture and, in 2019, I launched Hope Springs Gardening. I attend retreats and run courses helping other bereaved parents discover the simple joy of planting something and helping it to grow. I bring along a pot and some earth for everyone, and sometimes we plant a pot full of spring bulbs or herbs for the summer. The idea is that you have something to look forward to, when you don't want to look forward to anything. I always tell bereaved parents about Miranda and how I was once like them – a broken pot, who, ten years later, has been put back together again. I talk of hope, mindfulness, healing and the pleasure of getting your hands in the soil, working with nature and the cycle of life and death. Doing something active, being present. I am always rewarded by how much bereaved parents tell me they enjoy the sessions and feel proud of the many gardens and plants I know are being lovingly nurtured and tended by bereaved parents all over the country and beyond.

'It is hard work, but it is also my privilege to do it because Miranda is always at the centre of it.'

Working for Change

The death of a child is always an injustice. Whether it is because of a tragic accident, a medical condition or a crime, part of the huge disbelief and frustration that is felt by their parents when a child dies can often be linked to a social problem or a need for greater research or investment. These problems give many bereaved parents a chance to focus their energy and create positive change in the world.

For example, after four teenage boys died in a car crash in 2023, the mother of one of the boys who was 17 at the time, launched a campaign to introduce a law that would stop new drivers under 21 from having passengers of a similar age in their car for the first six months. Similarly, when her 15-year-old daughter died from taking MDMA, a mum campaigned to make it a specific offence to supply drugs to children under 16. Another mum whose son died campaigned to allow parents to be able to access their children's social media accounts.

Some bereaved parents find it helpful to be able to focus on the reason their child died and try to ensure that, as much as possible, it doesn't affect anyone else. The need to know that their child's death was not in vain is extremely strong.

Liz's son, Will, was 20 years old when he died after being struck by a car while riding his bike. Liz and her husband knew that Will was on the organ donor register and agreed that they wanted nothing of Will to be wasted; if he could help someone else live then that would give them some comfort. His organs helped 12 people to live and improved the sight of four others. But although they had ticked the box on the many forms to say they would like to hear from the people who had received Will's organs, they only received one thank you, from the mother of a two-year-old who had received part of Will's liver.

The lack of correspondence from the donor families made Liz question what the guidelines were for people receiving donor organs and took her and her family on a journey of discovery about the process of donating and receiving organs:

> 'I wondered if there was a clear reason why so few wrote thank you notes when it clearly meant so much to the donor families. After some research, I was surprised to learn that the only information recipients of organs received when they left the hospital was an impersonal leaflet included in their discharge notes. The leaflet's opening sentence said recipients could write to their donor if they wanted to but that there was "no pressure".
>
> 'There was no training for medical staff on how to discuss the donor or how to say thank you to the donor's families. Understandably, recipients' and donors' identities needed to remain anonymous.

But did this mean donor families couldn't expect a thank you?

'The NHS asked if I would help shape a better experience for donor families and try to increase the number of thank you letters being sent by recipients. So we launched "Don't Forget the Donor", a campaign to help raise awareness among organ recipients and their medical support staff, about why it is important to communicate with the bereaved families, who need to know their loved one's life made a difference.

'We agreed on an ambitious target of encouraging up to 75 per cent of recipients to write thank you letters over the next three years. We knew that there was no such thing as an "ungrateful" recipient, but not knowing what or how to say it, or worrying about upsetting the donor family were among the key reasons for not communicating. We came up with a plan to educate recipients, their nurses and donor families on why it is important to write, and to help recipients feel confident in expressing their feelings. I travelled up and down the country to a number of NHS training courses for recipient nurses telling Will's story. On those long train journeys, I reflected that Will would have loved to have known that he was making a change.

'The process was slow, but we rewrote leaflets, built new websites and created guidelines for nursing staff on how they should speak to recipients.

'Since Will's death, the law has been changed. Now, we are all automatically part of the organ donation scheme. I'm incredibly proud of what we have achieved, both with "Don't Forget the Donor" and the Will Houghton Foundation, which works with UK charities to help 14- to 24-year-olds reach their potential through education and sport.

'Ultimately, everything we do is an excuse for me to keep on talking about Will.'

Finding and Creating New Perspectives on Grief

To grieve for a child is to find yourself on a learning curve you never wanted to be on. Whether it is learning about a particular disease or a danger they were not aware of before their child died, or simply learning about the experience of grief itself, many bereaved parents and siblings can find themselves becoming experts in areas that they never wanted to be, and which are often poorly served in terms of information and resources.

Some bereaved parents find themselves motivated to share what they have learned in a creative way, either by writing their own books, or scripts, about their particular experience and the way in which their child's death impacted them. Others may choose to write songs, make films or start podcasts to raise awareness and engage with particular audiences. (The films *The Danger Age* and *Death at Birth* are both examples of films created by bereaved parents to help raise awareness.) Others find innovative ways to honour their child's passions by establishing events, awards and new networks to inspire other children and their families. Below are a few examples which you may find useful.

The Iris Project

theirisproject.org

The Iris Project was established by Ben Goldsmith and his former wife Kate Rothschild after the death of their daughter Iris when she was 15. Honouring Iris's love of the natural world, animals and the sea, the project supports and celebrates young people who are working to protect and restore their local natural environment. At the heart of the project is the Iris Prize, which rewards both new ideas and established projects run by young people who are championing nature around the world. Ben also wrote a memoir of his experience when Iris died, *God is An Octopus* – details are on page 177.

The DSM Foundation

dsmfoundation.org.uk

Fiona Spargo-Mabbs established a drug education charity, the DSM Foundation, after her son, Daniel, died after taking ecstasy when he was 16 years old. The foundation provides drug education resources and programmes, and commissioned a playwright, Mark Wheeller, to write a play about Daniel's story and help other young people to make choices that would keep them safe around drugs. The play – *I Love You, Mum – I Promise I Won't Die* – was published by Bloomsbury and has been studied, taught and performed in schools, colleges and community youth theatres across the UK and beyond (see page 90 for details).

The Danger Age

When his son Conwy, two, drowned in a tragic accident, Simon set about raising funds to create this short film, directed by Brad Williams. He wanted to highlight the unique vulnerability of children between two and four years old in order to help prevent future tragedies. Simon said: 'My hope is that, by everyone watching the film and spreading the word, we can somehow help to prevent future accidents.' *The Danger Age* can be seen on the ALMT website, see page 171, or by searching the title on YouTube.

The Student Grief Network (SGN)

studentgriefnetwork.co.uk

Anna May's little brother, Benny, died when she was ten years old. When her father died during her final year at university, she decided to establish the SGN, acknowledging the impact of bereavement on students who are studying away from home. The SGN addresses the challenges of bereavement for students and holds regular meetings and workshops, providing students with space for connection, creativity and empowerment.

The Red Hand Files

theredhandfiles.com

> 'Over the years, The Red Hand Files has burst the boundaries of its original concept to become a strange exercise in communal vulnerability and transparency.'
>
> **Nick Cave**

Nick Cave, whose sons Arthur, 15, and Jethro, 30, died 7 years apart, started the Red Hand Files as a way of directly answering his fans' questions. The simple website has become a popular and comforting resource for a wide audience, especially the bereaved and those facing death in many forms.

Starting a Charity

> 'The best way to find yourself is to lose yourself in the service of others.'
>
> **Mahatma Gandhi**

Another way in which bereaved parents continue to parent their child is by setting up a charity, trust or organisation in their name. The death of a child is a unique experience and one that only that child's parent can ever claim to have gone through, and the knowledge they can survive their child's death means they can survive the very worst thing life has to offer. Some parents find they can use this unique experience to create new charities that help many more people. Helping others who may have faced similar challenges or experienced the same illness as your child, helping to raise awareness of and pay for funding towards making the lives of others better, is a powerful way to feel that your child's death has not been in vain, and to leave a lasting legacy in the world that reaches beyond your lifetime.

It has been my privilege to work with and support many charities, all established by families I have supported. Below is a small selection of them, which you may find inspirational or helpful for you in grief. There is also information about the Angus Lawson Memorial Trust (ALMT), the charitable trust which has funded this book, on page 170.

Grayson's Legacy Support Trust

graysonslegacysupport.co.uk

Grayson's Legacy Support Trust was established by his parents, Craig and Faye, after their baby Grayson, who was ten months old, died of a rare disease called Acute Necrotising Encephalopathy of Childhood (ANE). A healthy little boy, he became very poorly at home and his parents rushed him to hospital. It was at the start of the coronavirus pandemic of 2020, and the strict social distancing rules in place at the time meant his parents had very little access to their son, even when he was moved overnight to a different hospital. When he died after just a few days, they had no information about what had happened to their baby or what had caused his death and were sent home with just a few leaflets to support them.

Their experience and deep love for their son inspired them to create Grayson's Legacy Trust, a charity funding research into ANE and other rare diseases.

Faye said:

> 'We were sent home, without our baby and just a few leaflets on "what to do after a death". None of which we could do anyway, because the country was put into a strict lockdown. With all but a few

keywords that we somehow managed to hold on to, we started researching to try to understand what and why this had happened. We founded Grayson's Legacy Support Trust to provide a safe space for other bereaved families, fundraise and collaborate with charities supporting and raising awareness for ANE and other rare diseases. Our mission is to achieve earlier diagnosis of ANE for children, and reduce the number of deaths it causes.

'Everything we do, we do for Grayson. There just aren't the words to describe how much we miss him, how much we love him. He is our everything and the reason that we keep going.'

SUDC UK

sudc.org.uk

Nikki Speed set up SUDC UK in 2017. Her daughter, Rosie, died in 2013, when she was a completely healthy, very much loved, two-year-old. Nikki has a PhD in biochemistry and combined her scientific background with her experience as a bereaved parent to co-found SUDC UK, a charity that is dedicated to raising awareness, funding research and supporting families affected by SUDC. Nikki has trained thousands of professionals, directly supported hundreds of suddenly bereaved family members, and is now an active member of child death overview panels in England, the All-Party Parliamentary Group for bereavement and the Child Bereavement Network.

Amy Robinson Foundation

amyrobinsonfoundation.org

Laura and Kieran Robinson set up the Amy Robinson Foundation after the sudden and unexplained death in 2022 of their precious daughter Amy when she was three years old. The foundation offers grants to bereaved families to access therapy from professionals experienced in dealing with child bereavement. Grants can be used towards counselling and other forms of bereavement support including art therapy, play therapy, EMDR and CBT.

Horatio's Garden

horatiosgarden.org.uk

Olivia and David Chapple founded Horatio's Garden after their 17-year-old son Horatio died in 2001. Horatio was on expedition in the Norwegian archipelago of Svalbard and his camp was attacked by a polar bear. Horatio had recently volunteered at the Duke of Cornwall Spinal Treatment Centre in Salisbury during his school holidays and, while there, had suggested the patients would benefit from more outside space. Horatio's Garden was established and the charity has since built a series of beautiful, award-winning gardens in a number of spinal units around the country, providing a vibrant and nurturing sanctuary to patients recovering after spinal injuries, and improving mental health and well-being. The aim is to eventually have Horatio's Gardens in all 11 spinal injury units in the UK.

SLOW (Surviving the Loss of Your World)

slowgroup.co.uk

Nicola Whitworth co-founded SLOW after the death of her daughter, Naomi, in 2005. SLOW connects grieving parents and provides regular meetings for bereaved parents and siblings where families can take strength from the support of others. The charity also runs creative workshops for bereaved children and provides support for professionals.

Rosie's Rainbow Fund

rosiesrainbowfund.co.uk

Rosie's Rainbow Fund was set up in 2004 by bereaved mum Carolyn Maylin. Her daughter Rosie died in 2003 when she was 11 after spending many months in hospital being treated for a rare illness. While in hospital, Rosie, who enjoyed the performing arts, expressed a wish to raise money to help other children undergoing lengthy hospital stays. Rosie's Rainbow Fund now supports sick and disabled children and their families with music and other therapies in hospitals, schools and the community.

Teddy's Wish

teddyswish.org

Jen and Chris Reid set up Teddy's Wish after their first child Edward died suddenly and unexpectedly in his cot when he was three months old. Teddy's Wish now provides bereavement counselling and support for families grieving the loss of a baby, and funds vital research into the causes of SIDS, stillbirth and neonatal death.

The Tom Love Trust

tomlovetrust.com

Geoff and Debs Love set up The Tom Love Trust after their son Tom died in Africa in 2022. The trust works in partnership with the ALMT to support children and young people in deprived areas of the UK and Africa – places close to Tom's heart – aiming to instil a sense of adventure and inspire them to follow their passions.

Footprints Baby Loss

footprintsbabyloss.org

Footprints Baby Loss was set up by two mums, Suzie Schofiled and Sharon Darke, who both experienced the premature birth and death of twin babies. The charity provides vital support to parents and families who have experienced this complex and unique death, of one or more of their twins or triplets before, during or after birth.

The achievements of the parents I mention here are only a few examples of bereaved parents everywhere who go on to make changes and help others in the name of their child. And for every parent who has set up a charity or run a marathon or campaigned for a new law, there are just as many who choose to live quietly and privately with their child's memory. There is no gold standard, no better or worse way to honour your child's life, and it is not ever your responsibility to rush out and change the world because your child has died. However, even those who don't make outwardly visible gestures have shown me that a child's death often creates a new energy within them; many bereaved parents say they develop an inner strength, one they never wanted or asked to possess, and yet nonetheless now carry with them throughout their lives.

In the 1990s, psychologists Richard Tedeschi, PhD, and Lawrence Calhoun, PhD, developed the concept of 'post-traumatic growth', the idea that people who endure psychological struggle following adversity can often see positive personal growth afterwards, developing a better understanding of themselves and how to live. The children's author Mark Lemon puts it more simply, describing his grief as a 'superpower' that has given him strength and helped him to move on in life. Many bereaved parents talk of being able to see the world through new eyes, with greater clarity and a better sense of what matters in life – of stressing less about the small things and cherishing life's simple pleasures.

However your grief comes to you and however you find yourself carrying it, whether that means jumping out of a plane to raise money or planting a few bulbs in a pot on the windowsill, you may find that it teaches you something about yourself, your own limits and capabilities, strengths and weaknesses, that other experiences can never teach you. It opens a door that only you can walk through, to a room only you can find. Like the child you are grieving, it is uniquely yours, and always will be.

About the Angus Lawson Memorial Trust (ALMT)

'No man stands so tall as when he stoops to help a child.'

Abraham Lincoln

The Angus Lawson Memorial Trust was founded to create a lasting legacy for Angus Lawson, who died in 2006 when he was two years old. Angus's father, Nick, was touched by the incredible kindness shown to him by so many people after his son's death. He wanted to reflect this by creating a trust that would have the same kindness at its heart and make a positive impact on children's lives everywhere.

Now known as the ALMT, the trust has one simple but ambitious aim: to improve the quality of life for disadvantaged children and young people around the world. The ALMT is run by a board of highly experienced trustees, who assess and award grants to grassroots charities and projects that align with the trust's vision. The ALMT is particularly interested in supporting early intervention initiatives that address the root causes of inequality and actively find solutions to proven problems affecting children. With the trust's origins always front of mind and the support of Jenni Thomas, OBE, as the ALMT's patron, projects providing bereavement support and palliative care for children and their families are always of particular significance.

Since 2006, the ALMT has funded over 350 projects in 38 countries, and developed partnerships with outstanding charitable organisations and individuals who are working to make the world a better place. Projects the ALMT supports are diverse and wide-ranging in their scope but share a common aim of achieving lasting change.

A commitment to due diligence, along with the collective experience, insight and compassion of the ALMT's trustees, has helped to form a growing network of like-minded donors who help to raise money and continue funding the vital projects that make such a difference to children everywhere.

For more information about the ALMT and the projects, and to find out how you can support its work, visit the ALMT website: almt.org

Useful Information

Legal Information and Advice

Citizen's Advice Bureau | citizensadvice.org.uk
Confidential and free advice on health matters, benefits, legal proceedings, witness service and much more.

Government Services and Information | gov.uk
For all current legal information on the law around death and illness, including entitlement to benefits and parental leave when a child dies, as well as details on the financial support available for funerals.

Charities and Organisations

Amy Robinson Foundation | amyrobinsonfoundation.org
Offers grants to bereaved families to access counselling and other forms of bereavement support including art therapy, play therapy, EMDR and CBT.

Antenatal Results & Choices | arc-uk.org
Impartial information and support to help you decide on your next steps when a pregnancy is complicated.

British Association for Counselling and Psychotherapy (BACP) | bacp.co.uk
The professional association and register for members of the counselling professions in the UK.

British Pregnancy Advisory Service | bpas.org
Healthcare charity supporting women and couples who decide to end a pregnancy.

Child Bereavement UK | childbereavementuk.org
Support for children and young people, and their families, when a child grieves or dies.

Child Funeral Charity | childfuneralcharity.org.uk
For help with paying for funeral expenses.

Cruse Bereavement Support | cruse.org.uk
The UK's largest charity for bereavement support and information.

David Trickey | davidtrickey.com
Resources, guidance and information for parents and professionals from the leading consultant clinical psychologist David Trickey, who works with traumatised children and their families, particularly following traumatic bereavement.

Drinkaware | drinkaware.co.uk
Advice, information and tools to help people make better choices about their drinking.

Footprints Baby Loss | footprintsbabyloss.org
Support for parents and families who experience the death of one or more of their twins or triplets.

Frank | talktofrank.com
Honest advice and information about drugs for young people and their families.

Grayson's Legacy Support Trust | graysonslegacysupport.co.uk
Fundraising, collaboration and support to raise awareness for ANE and other rare diseases.

Humanists UK | humanists.uk
For help and information about creating your funeral service.

Institute of Civil Funerals | iocf.org.uk
For help finding an approved funeral celebrant.

Rosie's Rainbow Fund | rosiesrainbowfund.co.uk
Music therapy for very sick and disabled children and their families in hospitals, schools and the community.

Royal College of Pathologists | rcpath.org
Information and guidelines about pathology and autopsy in the UK.

Samaritans | samaritans.org
Support for people bereaved by suicide and anyone who is struggling to cope.

SAMM | samm.org.uk
For support for anyone bereaved after murder and manslaughter.

SANDS | sands.org.uk
Support for anyone who has been affected by pregnancy loss or the death of a baby before, during or shortly after birth.

SLOW (Surviving the Loss of Your World) | slowgroup.co.uk
Groups and individual support for bereaved parents and siblings.

SUDC (Sudden Unexplained Death in Childhood) UK | sudc.org.uk
Support and information after the sudden, unexplained death of a child.

Survivors of Bereavement by Suicide (SOBS) | uksobs.com
Peer-to-peer support for all those over the age of 18 impacted by suicide loss in the UK.

Teddy's Wish | teddyswish.org
Bereavement counselling, support and information for grieving families following the death of a baby.

The Angus Lawson Memorial Trust | almt.org
Grants and funding for organisations working to improve the lives of children and young people worldwide.

The Child Bereavement Network | childbereavementnetwork.org.uk
A hub for professionals working with bereaved children, young people and their families.

The Compassionate Friends | tcf.org.uk
Support for bereaved parents, siblings and grandparents who have experienced the death of a child of any age (from one month old to an adult son or daughter) and from any cause.

The Coroners' Courts Support Service | coronerscourtssupportservice.org.uk
Emotional support and practical help from trained volunteers for bereaved families, witnesses and others attending an inquest at a Coroner's Court.

The Lullaby Trust | lullabytrust.org.uk
Support for families who experience the sudden loss of a baby or young child.

The Miscarriage Association | miscarriageassociation.org.uk
Help for anyone affected by miscarriage, molar pregnancy or ectopic pregnancy.

The Ruth Strauss Foundation | ruthstraussfoundation.com
Support for families facing the death of a parent to cancer.

The Student Grief Network (SGN) | studentgriefnetwork.co.uk
Supporting students who are dealing with grief, softening the impact of bereavement in universities.

The UK Sepsis Trust (UKST) | sepsistrust.org
Information and support for anyone bereaved by sepsis.

UK Trauma Council | uktraumacouncil.org
Free, evidence-based resources and guidance on traumatic bereavement for professionals and carers supporting children under 18.

Winston's Wish | winstonswish.org
Support for children, teenagers and young adults (up to the age of 25) who experience the death of a parent or guardian.

Books

The following books have all been recommended by bereaved parents:

A Heartbeat Away: Finding hope after grief and loss by Flappy Lane Fox (Child Bereavement Trust, 2005)

A Heart that Works by Rob Delaney (Coronet, 2023)

Always a Sibling: The forgotten mourner's guide to grief by Annie Sklaver Orenstein (Hachette Go, 2024)

Ask Me His Name by Elle Wright (Lagom, 2019)

Beyond Tears: Living after losing a child by Ellen Mitchell (Saint Martin's Griffin, 2009)

Faith, Hope and Carnage by Nick Cave and Seán O'Hagan (Canongate Books, 2023)

How to Survive the Loss of a Child: Filling the emptiness and rebuilding your life by Catherine M Sanders PhD (Prima Publishing, 1992)

If Not for You by Georgina Lucas (Little, Brown, 2022)

*I Love You, Mum – I Promise I Won't Di*e by Mark Wheeller (Bloomsbury Methuen Drama, 2017)

I Wasn't Ready to Say Goodbye: Surviving, coping and healing after the sudden death of a loved one by Brook Noel and Pamela D Blair, PhD (Sourcebooks, 2008)

The Death of a Child edited by Peter Stanford (Bloomsbury, 2011)

When It Is Darkest: Why people die by suicide and what we can do to prevent it by Rory O'Connor (Vermilion, 2021)

For professionals

An Acquaintance with Death – Memoirs of a Paediatrician by Dr Richard G Wilson (Troubador, 2025)

Bereaved Children and Teens edited by Earl A. Grollman (Beacon Press, 1995)

Grief in Children by Atle Dyregrov (Jessica Kingsley Publishers, Ltd., 2008)

Loss, Change and Grief: An educational perspective by Erica Brown (David Fulton Publishers, 2016)

For children

Badger's Parting Gifts by Susan Varley (Andersen Press, 1987)

God Is an Octopus: Loss, love and a calling to nature by Ben Goldsmith (Bloomsbury Wildlife, 2023)

Michael Rosen's Sad Book by Michael Rosen and Quentin Blake (Walker Books, 2011)

The Paper Dolls by Julia Robinson and Rebecca Cobb (Macmillan Children's Books, 2013)

Missing Mummy by Rebecca Cobb (Macmillan Children's Books, 2012)

What Does Dead Mean? by Caroline Jay and Jenni Thomas OBE (Jessica Kingsley Publishers, 2012)

The Invisible String by Patrice Karst and Joanne Lew-Vriethoff (Litte, Brown Young Readers, 2018)

Acknowledgements

People often wonder if a career in bereavement support isn't rather sad, but the truth is I have been very fortunate to meet and work alongside some of the kindest, brightest and most talented people throughout my career and during the writing of this book.

With that in mind, I would first like to say a very big thank you to my co-writer Sarah Thompson, who has helped me tell my story, captured the experiences of bereaved parents and tackled an enormously difficult subject matter with such empathy and finesse. It has been a wonderful experience working together, Sarah.

I must also thank the National Health Service, for giving me a career and encouraging and enabling me to make systemic changes and develop the bereavement services that changed the way grieving families are supported. Thank you also to all the NHS colleagues and professionals who I worked with for over 50 years, both in the Buckinghamshire NHS Trust and at Oxford Regional Health Authority, in particular Chief Nurse Executive Heather Cawthorn, and Sister Jean Macdonald, MBE.

I'm also very grateful to all the doctors, nurses, midwives, clinical psychologists, counsellors and therapists who have helped, inspired and mentored me in my work, in particular but not limited to: John Bowlby, Dr Donald Garrow, Dr Dermod MacCarthy, Dr Kim Cheetham, Dr Alison Earley and Sir Muir Gray, Dr Richard Wilson, Robin Skynner, Arturo Ezquerro,

Dr Diana Riley, Marianne de Groot, Vicki Allanach, Tracey Martin and Donna Ockenden.

Thank you to everyone behind my Nye Bevan Award in 2000 and my OBE in 2002, especially Susan Tunnard at the Prince's Trust. These awards, as well as being entirely unexpected, were extremely valuable in helping to publicise and raise awareness of bereavement work everywhere. I am also very proud and honoured to have received an Honorary Doctorate from Buckinghamshire New University in 2007, in recognition of a lifetime's work for the NHS and the Child Bereavement charity.

Thanks and much appreciation also to Dr Geoffrey and Mrs Kate Guy, Linda Wyatt, Patti Horrocks, Rachel Carter and Claire Middleton for their generous and constant support in the early days. Thanks to my goddaughter Rebecca Cobb, who illustrated *Missing Mummy*, and also to Brad Williams, who produced the award-winning short film, *The Danger Age*, that did so much to raise awareness and can be seen on YouTube and my website. Also to Nick Heath for producing my podcast *Jenni Thomas Talks About Child Bereavement* which can all be accessed on the ALMT website and to Will and Caroline Greenwood. And thank you especially to Vanessa Cummings, who has worked with me since joining the Child Bereavement Trust team as a project manager in 1997. I could not have managed then or now without her valuable help and friendship. And to my great friend Nic Whitworth, founder of SLOW, who has taught me so much as together we have enjoyed the challenge of co-facilitating our 'Reflect, Restore and Renew' bereavement retreats for the past 16 years.

Very special, heartfelt thank yous to my dear friends Kara and Nick Lawson. Kara, you are a wise and trusted confidante and sounding board. And Nick, thank you for recognising the importance of this work, and supporting so many bereaved parents through this book. Thank you to all the trustees of The Angus Lawson Memorial Trust; to Silvie Wallington for her sensitive illustrations; and to Rebecca Pirt who has worked so hard behind the scenes to make this book happen. Deepest gratitude also to Stuart Roden for his ongoing support; I wouldn't be writing this without it. Thanks also to Julia Kellaway for her deft and wise edits, and to my talented niece, Amy Fennell, for my fabulous author photo.

Enormous amounts of love and thanks to all of my children: my eldest son Gavin, who takes such interest in my work and designed my website jennithomas.com, and my eldest daughter Claudine, who is a constant source of fun and loving support and always makes me laugh. To her younger sister Little Jenn who works so hard, and manages to stay so close even from Italy. Thank you, Jenn, for also being my trusted proofreader. I'm especially grateful to Jenn and her brother Darren; you both taught me so much about being bereaved from when I first met you as little children and became your mum, and you continue to do so even now. I am also deeply grateful for the very special experience of being a granny (or Rara) to my 11 grandchildren. My love and thanks also to my thoughtful, kind sisters, Shirl and Les – life simply wouldn't be the same without you both.

And lastly but by no means least, to the many, many bereaved parents and families who have shared their precious children with me over the last 60 years. No one has taught me so much about love, life and courage as you. Thank you.

About the Author

Jenni Thomas, OBE, is a bereavement and grief counsellor with over 60 years' experience working with and supporting the parents, siblings and other family members of children who have died. Born in 1943 in South Africa, Jenni moved to England in 1952 with her family and joined the NHS as a nursery nurse in 1961. Jenni pioneered child bereavement care and was the first bereavement counsellor in the NHS. She is also the founder of Child Bereavement UK and has trained thousands of nursing, medical and other public sector professionals. She has received numerous awards, including the Nye Bevan Lifetime Achievement award for her work as Paediatric and Maternity Bereavement Facilitator and an OBE in recognition of her work. She is the author of many bereavement care training guides, as well as the book *What Does Dead Mean?* and the podcast series *Jenni Thomas Talks About Child Bereavement*. Today, Jenni is the bereavement counsellor for and patron of the Angus Lawson Memorial Trust. She has four children and eleven grandchildren. Jenni lives in Marlow, Buckinghamshire. For more information visit: jennithomas.com

Sarah G. Thompson is a non-fiction author whose titles include *Happy Single Mother* and *Style Council: Inspirational Interiors in Ex-Council Homes*. She's also the ghostwriter behind a number of bestselling celebrity memoirs and a journalist whose work has appeared in national newspapers. Sarah has lived in Birmingham and London, and now lives in Bridport, West Dorset, with her two teenage children. For more information visit: sarahgthompson.com

Printed in Dunstable, United Kingdom

67634747R00112